INDEX INVESTING AND EXCHANGE-TRADED FUNDS

INDEX INVESTING AND EXCHANGE-TRADED FUNDS

FUNDS

A Handbook for Stockbrokers and Asset Managers in Nigeria

First published 2024

ISBN: 978 978 771 781 3

Acknowledgments

Writing this book has been a fulfilling experience, and I am deeply grateful to everyone who has contributed to its creation.

First and foremost, I would like to express my sincere gratitude to the Group CEO/Co-founder of Vetiva Capital Management Limited, Mr. Chuka Eseka, whose mentorship has been invaluable. His willingness to support my foray into the world of Exchange-Traded Funds and provide feedback has significantly enriched this book. I would also like to thank Mrs. Oyelade Eigbe, my colleague and friend, for helping to refine this text with meticulous attention to detail.

To Dr. Olaolu Mudasiru ("Dr. Bob"), even beyond your time on earth, your unwavering belief in me continues to resonate in my life. This book is, in part, a tribute to the profound influence you have had on my journey. Thank you for all that you gave.

I am grateful to the CEO of the NGX, Mr. Jude Chiemeka, for his guidance throughout this process. I would also like to appreciate the following for the practical insights offered in the process of writing this book - Mr. Bola Ajomale (FCA, FCS, M.IoD) Executive Commissioner, Operations, Securities and Exchange Commission, Nigeria, Mr. Aigbovbioise Aig-Imoukhuede, President of the Fund Managers Association of Nigeria and Managing Director of Coronation Asset Management Limited, and Mr. Oluropo Samuel Dada, FCS, President / Chairman of Council, Chartered Institute of Stockbrokers and Chief Executive Officer/ Co-Founder of Network Capital Limited.

I thank my family and friends for their unwavering support and encouragement throughout this project. Your belief in me has been a constant source of motivation.

Lastly, I want to thank my readers for the interest in learning more about Exchange-Traded Funds. I hope this book serves as a valuable resource and inspires a deeper understanding of the subject.

Damilola Ajayi
November 2024

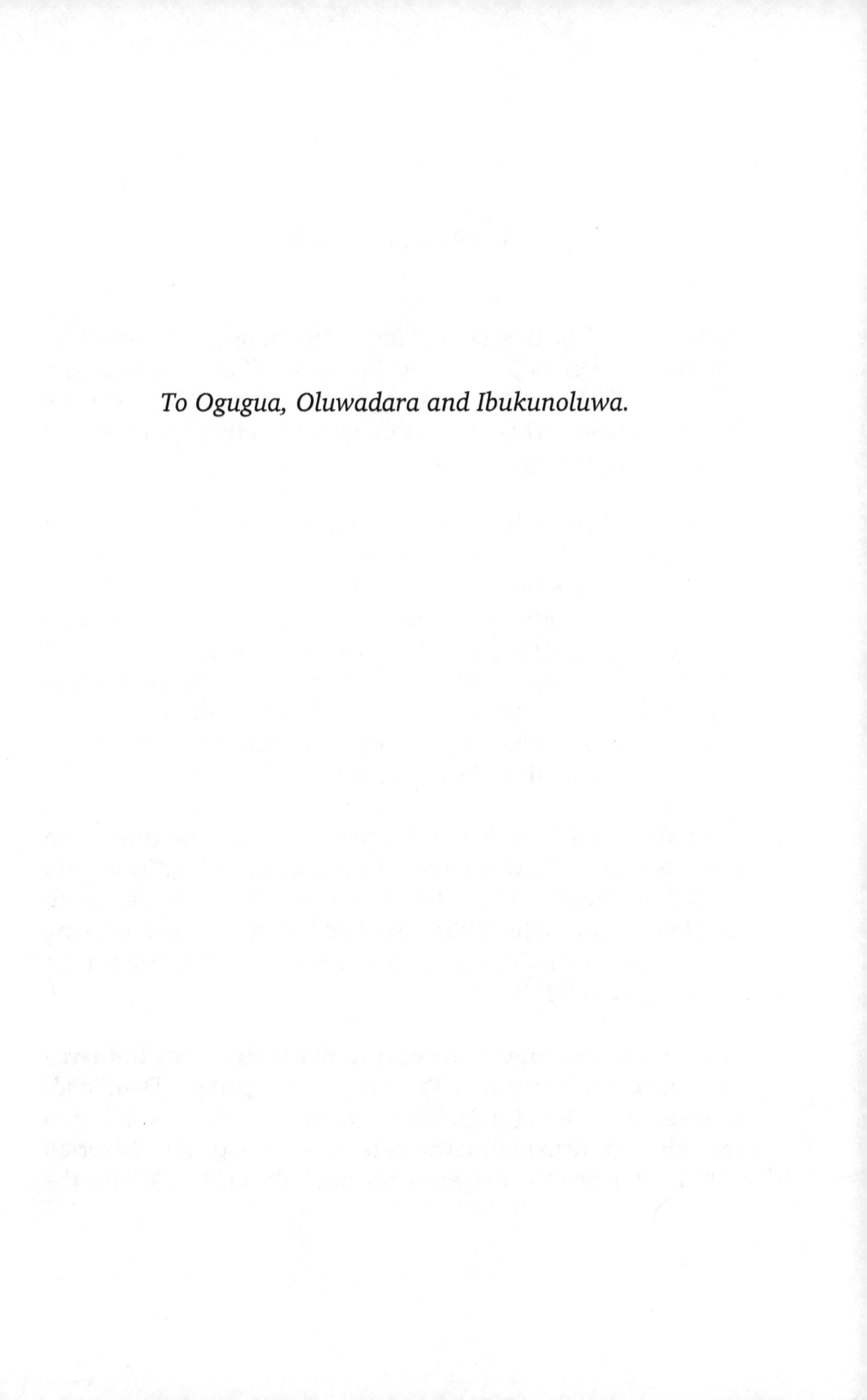

To Ogugua, Oluwadara and Ibukunoluwa.

Foreword

The arrival of this book, "Index Investing and Exchange-Traded Funds," couldn't be more fitting. While the concept of ETFs might seem established, the industry is truly hitting its stride. This revolution, ignited in the 1990s, is now experiencing a surge in popularity.

I have the distinct honor of introducing this book, authored by none other than Damilola Ajayi, the Executive Director/ Group Chief Operating Officer at Vetiva Capital Management Limited. As both a mentor and a leader, Damilola's expertise is unparalleled. For two decades, he has steered the ship of our asset management business, which includes Wealth Management & Institutional Sales, along with the Trust Division. His experience encompasses Investment Management, Equities Research, and Institutional Sales.

It is crucial to acknowledge that the ETF revolution rests upon the even more fundamental concept of indexing. This field applies efficient market theory and quantitative science to build portfolios. The author has had the privilege of working with pioneers in this space, and his personal journey with ETFs began in 2009.

A Personal Journey: Witnessing the Birth of an Industry
An encounter with an ETF prospectus sparked Damilola's interest in index (or passive) investing. This exploration led him to actively participate in shaping the Nigerian ETF landscape. He played a pivotal role in developing the

regulatory framework, crafting ETF rules, and even advising on the listing of the very first Nigerian ETF, the NewGold ETF. His leadership extended to subsequent listings, including the first equity ETF, the first bond ETF, and the first sector-focused equity ETFs in Nigeria.

A Dream for the Future

With the global ETF market reaching staggering heights, the Nigerian market, though nascent, holds immense potential. This book serves as Damilola's contribution to realizing this potential. He envisions a future where Nigeria's ETF market mirrors global standards in terms of product variety, sophistication, and liquidity.

Whether you are a seasoned investor, a curious broker, or an asset manager seeking to expand your offerings, this book is your indispensable guide. It's a clarion call for embracing a new investment paradigm – one focused on macro trends and thematic diversification, rather than the perils of single-stock selection. While the book delves deep into the world of ETFs and index investing, it does so with the understanding that the field is constantly evolving.

Within these pages, you will embark on a comprehensive exploration of ETFs. Understanding Indices (weighted and unweighted), the history of index investing and index funds, in-depth analysis of Exchange-Traded Funds, including their features, types, and emerging trends, utilizing ETFs for effective portfolio construction, asset allocation, diversification and rebalancing, the intricacies of structuring an ETF, including the ecosystem, listing process, index selection, creation and redemption mechanisms, cost considerations, trading strategies using ETFs, along with ETF pricing, settlement, and distributions.

The ETF Revolution: A New Era of Investing
ETFs have undeniably reshaped the investment landscape. Their lower fees, transparency, accessibility, and tax efficiency make them a compelling alternative to traditional mutual funds. Furthermore, their inherent liquidity fosters a dynamic trading environment where diverse investors can connect and participate in price discovery.

ETFs empower investors to adopt a top-down approach, facilitating asset allocation, sector rotation, and thematic investing. This shift encourages a focus on broader macroeconomic trends rather than individual stock picking.

The rise of ETFs has ushered in a new era of fee-based investment models, driven by a focus on fiduciary relationships between advisors and investors. This represents a fundamental shift in the financial industry.

As the ETF revolution continues to gain momentum, insightful and comprehensive education becomes paramount. This book serves as a powerful tool to navigate the complexities of this dynamic field and unlock the potential of index investing and ETFs.

I encourage you to delve into this book and empower yourself to be a part of this exciting new chapter in investing. I hope that this handbook empowers Nigerian investors to harness the full potential of ETFs and actively participate in the country's growing ETF market. Together, let's propel Nigeria's ETF industry towards a future that reflects global best practices.

Mr. Chuka Eseka
Group Chief Executive Officer
Vetiva Capital Management Limited Nigeria

Endorsements

I was excited to have been allowed a pre-read of this handbook on Exchange-Traded Funds (ETFs) written by Mr. Damilola Ajayi, partly because it's the start of building a digestible body of knowledge in a rapidly growing asset class.

Globally, ETFs have transformed how investors approach portfolio management, index investing, and tactical asset allocation. In Nigeria, the nascent ETF market promises significant potential for operators and investors to deepen the capital market, channel funds into investment opportunities, and smoothen the risk profiles of such investments. The handbook also directly aligns with global aspirations to increase financial education and inclusion among retail investors and operators such as stockbrokers, asset managers, and institutional investors.

For professionals, this handbook serves as a first step comprehensive guide for navigating the evolving ETF landscape. It provides the essential information required to structure an ETF and then deepens into testing scenarios, examining frameworks and rules. In addition, the handbook provides current information on the listing process and the role of ETFs in portfolio construction. After consulting this book, stockbrokers, asset managers, and financial professionals would be equipped to design and innovate new ETFs and capitalize on the immense opportunities available in

Nigeria. They would also be given a practical guide on how ETFs can be used to achieve efficient diversification and risk management.

The handbook correctly identifies that as technology continues to enable access to more data and quality information, there is a global shift toward index investing. It therefore, in light detail, explores the pros and cons of index-based strategies and explores the distinctions between passive and active investing approaches and how index methodologies influence ETF performance.

I particularly appreciate the illustrative examples to simplify complex concepts and the timely and relevant insights offered that both reflect global best practices and localized market dynamics. Each of the 5 well-articulated chapters is headed with a thoughtful quip such as *"There is a time to go long, a time to go short, and a time to go fishing."* to lighten the weight of the subject matter whilst setting the chapter theme.

I am pleased to conclude that this handbook will serve as a valuable practical guide to enhancing the investment strategies of investment professionals across Nigeria and assist them in unlocking the full potential of ETFs in this emerging market. I further believe this handbook will fill a gap in the preparation of aspiring asset managers, investment advisers, and students of the capital market in Nigeria.

Mr. Bola Ajomale (*FCA, FCS, M.IoD*)
Executive Commissioner, Operations
Securities and Exchange Commission, Nigeria

Damilola Ajayi is a consummate finance professional and I have known him for two decades. He is a leading subject matter expert in the Asset Management industry in West Africa having been one of the pioneers involved in the structuring and creating of the Exchange-Traded Products Market in Nigeria as far back as 2011. His depth of knowledge and eagerness to share and exchange insights with industry peers on the Exchange-Traded Funds (ETFs) is unparalleled.

Mr. Ajayi, through the Vetiva Fund Management team, has helped in no small measure to deepen the suite of products available on the Nigerian Exchange Limited (Formerly Nigerian Stock Exchange). The team currently manages five ETFs with a Total Net Asset Value of over Eight Billion naira (₦8 Billion) which is about 58% of the total Net Asset Value of Nigeria's ETF Industry. These products have helped investors (both retail and Institutional) diversify their risk and gain exposure to a basket of underlying stocks without directly investing in them.

I can boldly assert that there is no better person to author a book about ETFs in Nigeria than Mr. Ajayi who has been involved hands-on in structuring and maintaining various ETFs. This book, which is the first of its kind specifically curated for Nigeria's ETF space, would add so much value to literature and would be a reference point in many years to come in the Nigerian Investment industry. It could not have come at a better time, as the sector currently yearns for more products in the ETF market, as this would enhance the bouquet of investible products.

A deep dive into this book titled "Index Investing and Exchange-Traded Funds" shows that the author succinctly introduced the concept of passive/index investing, Index Funds, and the fundamentals of ETFs with clear practical examples. He delved into the concept of portfolio construction and how ETFs help with constructing optimal portfolios, (Risk and portfolio rebalancing were also covered in great depth).

This book covers the end-to-end process of structuring ETFs with well-thought-out examples. The author creatively discussed the concepts of trading ETFs on a recognized exchange like the Nigerian Exchange Limited (Formerly Nigerian Stock Exchange) and the benefits to investors (Payment of distributions).

As a finance professional myself with over 30 years of experience in the Capital Market, I endorse this book for Fund Managers, Stockbrokers, Investment professionals, and students who might want to make a foray into the ETF space either as investors or issuers. I enjoin the investment community in Nigeria to grab a copy, as this material does more than whet your investment appetite, it also covers enormous grounds on the subject matter of ETFs.

Mr. Jude Chiemeka
Chief Executive Officer
Nigerian Exchange Limited

In the intricate and evolving landscape of financial markets, the emergence of Exchange-Traded Funds (ETFs) has marked a pivotal shift, particularly in regions where traditional investment vehicles once dominated. The author, Damilola Ajayi's, journey into the world of ETFs, beginning with an exploration of the Satrix 40 BIT Prospectus during a business trip to South Africa, reflects the curiosity and dedication that are essential to understanding and harnessing the power of passive investing.

What stands out in this narrative is not just the acquisition of knowledge but the proactive approach to applying this understanding in the context of the Nigerian financial market. The fortuitous meeting with industry experts like Nerina Visser and the strategic developments at the Nigerian Stock Exchange (now NGX) underscore the author's commitment to innovation and growth within the investment management space.

As you delve into this book, you will find a wealth of insights drawn from real-world experiences and deep expertise. The author's ability to demystify complex financial instruments and present them in a way that is both engaging and informative is truly commendable. This work not only serves as a guide for those looking to understand ETFs but also as an inspiration for professionals across the investment management industry. I am confident that readers will find this book to be a valuable resource, one that will broaden their understanding of ETFs and their potential impact on the financial markets in Nigeria and beyond. The author's foresight in recognizing the significance of new asset classes and the importance of adapting to global financial trends and best practices is a testament of his commitment to the growth of the industry.

It is with great pleasure that I endorse this book and recommend
it to anyone interested in expanding their knowledge of ETFs
and their application in emerging markets.

Mr. Aigbovbioise Aig-Imoukhuede
President, Fund Management Association of Nigeria and
Managing Director of Coronation Asset Management Limited

I am delighted to endorse this well-researched document on an aspect of our securities market with so much potential and untapped opportunities.

The book *"Index Investing and Exchange-Traded Funds"* is a timely resource for the Nigerian Capital Market in helping market participants understand the intricacies of the evolving Exchange-Traded Products (ETPs) industry in Nigeria. No doubt, the Exchange-Traded Funds (ETFs) market in Nigeria is still in its infancy when compared with the Global Assets Under Management (AUM) for ETFs. As of today, the adoption of the product by investors has not yet reached the desired level. There is therefore, no gain saying that the production of this book will come in handy as a useful resource for all capital market operators looking to issue ETFs and play within the ETF space.

Since the listing of the first ETF on the Nigerian Exchange (NGX), the market has witnessed listings of other Exchange-Traded Products with more listings being expected.

As part of the team that developed rules and redemption framework for birthing the ETF industry in Nigeria, the author was able to painstakingly dissect the concept relating to index investing and ETFs using hypothetical worked examples while also drawing copiously from his extensive practical experience on the subject matter.

The book presents succinct highlights on the performance of indices globally and across known African exchanges. The author carefully holds out his position on the viability of index funds as investment products and the effectiveness of index investing. The features and different types of exchange-traded funds were analyzed to advance the author's view of the growth of the exchange-traded product industry as the single most disruptive trend within the asset management industry. The author delved into various ways in which ETFs can support the construction of optimal portfolios with relevant hypothetical examples to facilitate the reader's understanding. Stockbrokers, asset/fund managers and securities dealers will find the chapter on structuring an exchange-traded fund very informative as it details step by step, the creation and redemption process, structures, ecosystem, listing process, licensing and other relevant information about indices and ETFs. The book equally addressed issues relating to the trading of ETFs in terms of pricing, trade settlement, and distributions which will greatly benefit every market participant.

Subject to the author ensuring that all regulatory standards are duly adhered to in the course of publication, I confidently recommend the book as a useful resource in gaining a practical understanding of the dynamics of index and ETF products to every operator within the Nigerian capital market and beyond.

Mr. Oluropo Dada FCS
13th President & Chairman of Council
Chartered Institute of Stockbrokers and Chief Executive
Officer/Co-Founder of Network Capital Limited

Contents

Introduction

My Exchange-Traded Funds ("ETFs") journey started in 2009 when I came across the Satrix 40 ETF Prospectus (the ETF tracks the FTSE/JSE Top 40 Index) on a business trip to South Africa (on behalf of Vetiva). I was intrigued by the general concept of index (or passive) investing and took the time to study the Satrix 40 document in detail. Also, at that time, I had the opportunity to be introduced to Nerina Visser (Director at etfSA Portfolio Management Company). Nerina was able to explain ETF structures in detail and was very instrumental in opening my eyes to the world of ETFs.

Interestingly, around the same time, a new management team had resumed at the helm of affairs at the Nigerian Stock Exchange (Now Nigerian Exchange Group – "NGX") and in presenting a 5-year strategic plan to the market, the CEO of the Exchange, Oscar N. Onyema OON, communicated the objective of facilitating the listing of new asset classes on the Exchange starting with ETFs. Similarly, ABSA Capital (a South African Investment Bank) had communicated its intention to list an ETF in Nigeria. To ensure an appropriate regulatory framework was in place to support the listing, the Securities and Exchange Commission ("SEC") set up an ad-hoc committee to develop rules for ETF listings in Nigeria. I was privileged to be part of this initiative working with brilliant minds at the SEC and the NGX, amongst others, in developing

ETF rules for the Nigerian Market. In addition to this, a lot of work was done with the Central Securities Clearing System ("CSCS") team to come up with the Creation and Redemption framework for ETFs.

The listing of the NewGold ETF on the NGX (by ABSA Capital) in 2011 birthed the ETF industry in Nigeria. Vetiva acted as an adviser to the listing and the practical experience garnered in working with the ABSA team was invaluable. Following the NewGold ETF listing, I was privileged to lead a team of talented professionals at Vetiva Funds Managers Limited (the Asset Management subsidiary within the Vetiva Group) to develop and list the first equity ETF in Nigeria (the Vetiva Griffin 30 ETF), the first Bond ETF in Nigeria (the Vetiva S&P Nigerian Sovereign Bond ETF), and the first sector-focused Equity ETFs (the Banking, Consumer Goods and Industrials ETFs). I also had the opportunity to lead the advisory team that supported Lotus Capital Limited in the listing of the first Sharia-compliant ETF in Nigeria (the Lotus Halal Equity ETF) in 2014.

With Global Assets Under Management (AUM) for Exchange-Traded Funds estimated at $11.5trillion (PWC, 2024) as at the end of 2023 and expected to reach $14trillion by the end of 2024 (Blackrock, 2024), the ETF industry in Nigeria (currently at est. $10million AUM) has a long way to go. Nonetheless, with continuous capacity building, and awareness efforts by key stakeholders, the Nigerian ETFs market will attain the desired levels of investor adoption with time. I envision a future when our domestic ETFs market will reflect global standards in terms of product breadth, sophistication and relative liquidity. This handbook is my humble contribution towards the actualisation of this dream.

I am hopeful that this handbook will be a useful resource for Brokers, Asset Managers and other Finance professionals in Nigeria who are looking to issue ETFs and play within the ETF industry. It may also prove relevant to investors looking to practice index investing principles and/or introduce ETFs to their Portfolios.

Chapter 1

THE CONCEPT OF INDEX INVESTING

"By periodically investing in an index fund, the know-nothing investors can actually outperform most investment professionals." – Warren Buffett

1.1 Introduction

An appreciation of Exchange-Traded Funds, as investment products, will not be possible without a clear understanding of the concept of index investing, seeing that Exchange-Traded Funds became a reality on the basis of this concept. In this chapter therefore, we will drill down into the nature of indices and how they are constructed and computed, the meaning of index investing as a strategy, the history of index investing and its advantages and disadvantages. Over the years, the concept of index investing has had a profound impact on how investors build their portfolios and in this chapter, we will also discuss why index investing has become a popular strategy. Index investing is a commonly used term in the world of Portfolio Management and is frequently used interchangeably with the term "Passive Investing".

1.2 Understanding Indices

First and foremost, what is an index? (Plural: indices or indexes)

In its simplest form, indices are used to track or measure financial or economic data. A common example is the Consumer Price Index (CPI), which measures the change in the price of a basket of goods and services over time and is a common measure of inflationary trends within an economy. Another popular index is the London Interbank Offered Rate or "LIBOR" which was an interest rate index, but has now been phased out and replaced by the Secured Overnight Financing Rate ("SOFR"). It was arrived at by calculating the volume weighted median of repo transactions i.e., collateralised overnight borrowings.

We can also formally define indices, within the context of financial markets, as a group or basket of securities, derivatives, or other financial instruments that represent and measure the performance of a specific market, asset class, market sector, or investment strategy (S&P Dow Jones indices). Indices can also be used to track the performance of a group of assets (Chen, 2023) and are also used as a benchmark to monitor the performance of investment portfolios.

Some popular global indices are the Standard and Poor's 500 Index (S&P 500), which tracks the performance of the stocks of 500 of the largest companies listed on stock exchanges in the United States. Another is the Dow Jones Industrial Average Index, which is a price weighted index, and measures the daily stock price movements of 30 blue-chip companies listed on the Nasdaq and the New York Stock Exchange (covering all industries except transportation and utilities). In the United Kingdom, there is the FTSE 100 Index, which tracks 100 of the most highly capitalised stocks on the London Stock Exchange, whilst in Asia, the Nikkei 225, or the

Nikkei Stock Average, is a well-known benchmark index for the Tokyo Stock Exchange. The Nikkei Index is also a price weighted index like the Dow Jones index, and it measures the performance of 225 companies in Japan. In Africa, we have the FTSE/JSE Africa All Share Index, which is a broad market index that measures the performance of stocks listed on the Johannesburg Stock Exchange and the NGX All-Share Index, which tracks the general market movement of listed equities on the Nigerian Exchange.

Market	Broad Description
NGX All-Share Index	The NGX All-Share Index tracks the performance of all listed equities traded on the Nigerian Exchange.
Ghana Stock Exchange (GSE) Composite Index	The index tracks the performance of all listed equities traded on the Ghana Stock Exchange.
The BRVM Composite Index	The index tracks the performance of all listed equities traded on the Régionale des Valeurs Mobilières (BRVM). The BRVM is a regional stock exchange that serves 8 West African countries.

Fig. 1:1   Key stock market benchmark indices in West Africa

	2023	2022	2021	2020	2019
NGX All-Share Index	46%	20%	6%	50%	-15%
GSE Composite Index	28%	-12%	46%	-14%	-13%
BRVM Composite Index	5%	0.46%	39%	-9%	-8%

Performance of West African Benchmark Indices.

Source: *Vetiva Research*

The Concept of Index Investing
Indices can be used to capture a whole market (e.g., Equity, Fixed Income or commodity market) as we have with the NGX All-share Index, or a segment of the market e.g., a sector or industry. For example, in the US, we have the S&P 500® Financials which tracks companies within the S&P 500 but are financial sector companies based on Global Industry Classification Standards (*www.spglobal.com*). In West Africa, we also have sector indices such as the NGX Banking Index (Nigeria), the GSE Financial Stocks Index (Ghana) and the BRVM Finance Index (Francophone West Africa).

1.3   Weighted and Unweighted Indices
In the previous section, we referenced market capitalisation weighted and price weighted indices. What do these mean? In answering this question, we need to look at how indices are constructed. There are several steps involved in constructing an index but in general, index construction involves:

• Identifying the types of assets, industry, securities or markets to be tracked by the proposed index.

• Using a defined criteria to select the securities that will be included in the index based on (1) above. This can be based on asset class, security type, geography etc.

• Determining the criteria that will influence the impact that each component security will have on the index. This is what is called the weighting of a security in an index. Weightings are used as a means of placing emphasis on a particular factor e.g., size of the company or the share price of a company.

• Determining other relevant rules e.g., rebalancing rules, Cap on component weightings (if any) etc.

It is important to note that Indices can either be weighted (based on a particular factor such as value or price) or unweighted. In a weighted index, the component securities do not have the same relevance or impact in the computation of the index value. Examples of weighted indices are the NGX All-Share Index, the Ghana Stock Exchange Composite Index (GSE-CI) and the BRVM composite Index, which are weighted by market capitalisation. i.e. the higher the market capitalisation of a component security, the higher the weighting of the security in the Index. In an unweighted index however, each security has the same level of relevance or impact on the index. Unweighted indices are also known as equal-weighted indices (Connolly, 2013). An example of an unweighted index is the S&P 500 Equal Weight Index (EWI). The index was launched in 2003 and includes the same constituents as the capitalization weighted S&P 500, but each company in the S&P 500 EWI is allocated a fixed weight - or 0.2% of the index total at each quarterly rebalance (S&P Dow Jones Indices).

Worked example: Unweighted or equal-weighted indices:

A hypothetical index called the "Nigeria Unweighted Share Index" has 3 component stocks: Company A, Company B and Company C. What would be the return on the Index in 2023, if the constituent stocks posted the following returns in the same year:

Company A: 30%, Company B: 20%, and Company C: 10%?

Computation: For an unweighted or equal-weighted Index, the return of the index is the simple average of the returns of the component securities. Therefore, the return on the index will be calculated as:

Index Return = The sum of all the returns posted by the individual component securities divided by the number of securities in the index i.e. (30+20+10) / 3 = 20%.

1.4 Types of Weighted Indices

There are different types of weighted indices, which are based on the factor(s) that determine the relevance (weighting) given to each component security. Also, there are various categorization approaches for indices but for the purposes of this handbook, weighted indices are grouped under 3 categories which are:

- **Market Cap Weighted (or Value weighted):** In market cap-weighted or value weighted indices, a security's weighting within the index is based on its market value or market capitalisation. The market capitalisation of a company is the value of the company on the stock exchange. To compute the market value, the price of the security is multiplied by the number of units of the security that is listed. For example, if company A is priced at ₦2 (Two Naira) and has 10 (Ten) shares listed on a stock exchange, the market value is ₦2 multiplied by 10, which is ₦20 (Twenty Naira) Market capitalisation or Market Value.

Using a real-life company, the market capitalisation of Guaranty Trust Holding Company Plc. (which is listed on the NGX) as at

31st March, 2024, was ₦1,545,136,909,260.00 (One Trillion Five Hundred and Forty Five Billion, One Hundred and Thirty Six Million, Nine Hundred and Nine Thousand Two Hundred and Sixty Naira only), which is arrived at by multiplying the price of the stock i.e., ₦52.00 on the relevant date, by the total number of shares outstanding as at same date i.e., 29,431,179,224 units.

A Float-adjusted Market-capitalization Weighted Index is a variant of the market capitalisation weighting approach but with a "float factor" for each stock, which reflects the proportion of the outstanding shares that are freely held (*www.spglobal.com*).

- **Price-weighted:** In a price-weighted stock index, each security is weighted by its price per share, and the index is an average of the share prices of all the constituent companies in the index. An example of a price-weighted index is the Dow Jones Industrial Average in the US or the Nikkei Average in Japan. In a price-weighted stock index, each security is weighted by its price per share. Looking closely as price-weighted indices, we see that greater weight is given to stocks with higher prices in terms of their contribution to the index value. Some analysts consider this a disadvantage of price-weighted indices, but a clear advantage of this weighting method is the ease of calculating the index. To compute a price weighted index, the prices of all the component stocks is summed up and divided by an index divisor.

Worked Examples:

Question 1: A hypothetical index called "the Nigeria Price Weighted Index" has 3 component stocks. Company A, Company B and Company C. What would be the value of the index if each component stock has the following price?: Company A: ₦10 (Ten Naira), Company B: ₦20 (Twenty Naira), and Company C: ₦30 (Thirty Naira), if the index divisor is the number of constituent companies.

Computation:

The Nigerian Price Weighted Index value will equal the sum of component company stock prices divided by number of stocks, i.e., Index Value = (₦10 + ₦20 + ₦30) / 3 = 20

Question 2:   We are still on the hypothetical Index introduced in question 1. On the following day, the Company prices closed as follows: Company A – ₦20 (Twenty Naira), Company B – ₦30 (Thirty Naira), and Company C – ₦40 (Forty Naira). What is the return on the index?

Computation:

Step 1: compute the new index value i.e., Index Value = (₦20 + ₦30 + ₦40) / 3 = 30

Step 2: compute % change in index value i.e., (30/20) – 1= 50%

- **Fundamentally weighted index:** A fundamentally weighted index is one in which the weightings of the component securities are based on metrics or rules other than market capitalization or price. These metrics could be company revenues, earnings, or dividends (McCullough, 2018). Some analysts refer to fundamental indices loosely as strategic beta indices. Strategic beta can be explained as any index or related investment product that seeks to provide criteria to determine the weighting of the components of an index using a strategy other than conventional market-cap weighting strategies (*www.schwabassetmanagement.com*). An example of a fundamentally weighted index is The FTSE RAFI®. It derives its constituent weights from fundamental measures of company size e.g. cash flow, book value, total sales, and gross dividend to arrive at the weightings of the component securities (*www.ftserussell.com*). It should be noted that fundamentally weighted indices can track multiple metrics and assign a weighting or factor to each metric. Some analysts also include **Style indices** which capture various investor styles (growth, value, dividend yield) as part of fundamentally weighted indices. These indices are commonly used by active managers to benchmark a specific type of investing style (*moneyterms.co.uk*).

Worked Example: A hypothetical index called "the Nigeria Turnover Weighted index" assigns weightings in line with only one metric, the 5-year average annual turnover of each company. The index has 3 component stocks: Company A, Company B and Company C. What would be the weighting of each company in the Index if the component companies have the following 5-year average annual turnover: Company A – ₦50million, Company B – ₦30million and Company C – ₦20million

Computation: The weighting of each company would be the 5-year average annual turnover figure of the company divided by the total 5-year average annual turnover figure of all the companies represented in the index.

Step 1: The total 5-year average annual turnover figure is = ₦50m + ₦30m + ₦20m = ₦100m
Step 2: Weighting of company A = (50/100) * 100 = 50%, Weighting of company B = (30/100) * 100 = 30%, Weighting of company C = (20/100) * 100 = 20%

1.5 Index Divisors

An index divisor is a number used to divide the total market capitalisation of an Index to arrive at a predetermined Index value (called the base index value) on the date the index is launched. Subsequent values of the index are then compared to the base index value to arrive at the returns on the index. For example, The NGX All-Share Index was launched in January 1984 with a base value of 100. The Index divisor may be adjusted from time to time to account for changes to the index structure e.g. stock splits.

Example: A hypothetical stock market contains only 3 companies. Companies A, B, and C and you are asked to construct a value weighted index to track the performance of the broad market. Assume the Index was launched on the 31st of March 2024 with a starting index value of 1,000.

Question 1:
What index divisor would you use to achieve the intended index starting value?

Company Data

Stock	No. of shares	Price on 31st March 2024 (₦)
Company A	10,000	2.00 per share
Company B	20,000	5.00 per share
Company C	25,000	4.00 per share

Computation:

Stock	No. of shares	Share Price on 31 Mar.'24 (₦)	Market Capitalisation (₦)
Company A	10,000	2.00	20,000
Company B	20,000	5.00	100,000
Company C	25,000	4.00	100,000
Total Market Capitalisation (i)			**220,000**
Index Starting Value (ii)			**1,000**
Index divisor (iii) = (i) divided by (ii)			**220**

Question 2:

Compute the Index value on the 30th of June 2024 using the company data provided and index divisor computed in question 1 above. See below the pricing details of the stocks on 30th June 2024:

Stock	Price on 30th June 2024 (₦)
Company A	4.00 per share
Company B	3.00 per share
Company C	8.00 per share

Computation:

Stock	No of shares 2024	Share Price 30th June Market (₦)	Share Price Capitalisation (₦)
Company A	10,000	4.00	40,000
Company B	20,000	3.00	60,000
Company C	25,000	8.00	200,000
Total Market Cap (A)			300,000
Index Divisor (B) - *from solution in Q1*			220
Index Value - 30th June 2024 (C) = A÷B			**1,363.64**

Question 3:

What is the index performance in percentage terms between the 31st of March 2024 and the 30th of June 2024?

Computation:

Index Value on Date (X) – 31st March 2024 – 1,000
Index Value on Date (Y) – 30th June 2024 – 1,363.64

Percentage performance is (Index value on date Y minus index value on date X) divided by Index value on Date X) multiplied by 100.

i. e., ((1,363.64-1,000)/1,000) *100 = 36.36%

Question 4: What are the weightings of the index components as of 30th June, 2024?

Computation:

Stock	No of shares	Share Price 30th June 2024 (₦)	Market Capitalisation (₦)	Index Weighting (%) *
Company A	10,000	4.00	40,000	13.33
Company B	20,000	3.00	60,000	20.00
Company C	25,000	8.00	200,000	66.67
Total Market Capitalisation (A)			300,000	100%

Computed as market capitalisation of each company as a percentage of total market cap

1.6 What is Index Investing?

Index investing is a portfolio management strategy in which the investor buys assets with the intention of replicating the composition of an index such as the Standard and Poor's 500 Index (S&P500), the NGX All-Share Index, the GSE Composite Index or the BRVM Composite Index.

Passive investing is a portfolio strategy in which investor adopts a "buy-and-hold" approach to the management of a portfolio i.e., purchase of assets with the intention of holding such assets for a long period of time without "trading" the portfolio. According to the CFA Institute, Passive investing refers to any rules-based, transparent, and investable strategy that does not involve identifying mispriced individual securities. With these definitions, we see that the replication of an index is not technically required for a strategy to be termed "passive", even though most passive portfolios seek to track an index (Chen, 2020). **It is important to note however,**

that Index investing by its nature is a form of passive investment because portfolio constituents are not traded (except in specific circumstances e.g. during rebalancing) but are bought and held to mirror the composition of the relevant index.

There have been many questions over the years on the effectiveness of Index Investing. The notion that tracking an index can be an efficient use of capital seems counter-intuitive and investors, not just in Nigeria but globally have engaged in what is called the "Active vs Passive" conversation.

For context, what is active investing? Active Managers attempt to deliver returns that are superior to market returns through primarily selecting securities that are expected to outperform the market by studying and predicting market trends and positioning their portfolios accordingly.

Proponents of the active approach argue that passive investing is *"lazy investing"* as the Portfolio Manager makes little or no input to the performance of the portfolio. Also, index portfolios can only deliver an "average" return whereas active managers are able to take advantage of opportunities thrown up by markets from time to time to generate returns that outperform the average. That being said, proponents of index investing argue that active managers are tactical and as such the approach is expensive, thus eroding capital gains. Also, some argue that based on the efficient market hypothesis or efficient market theory, which assumes that all the information that can influence the price of an asset is available to all market participants at the same time, it is impossible to beat the market on a sustainable basis, and hence any attempts to beat an efficient market on an ongoing basis is futile.

My view on this conversation is simple. None of the approaches is a silver bullet and both approaches have their benefits and uses depending on specific portfolio circumstances. Also, it is important to note that based on the ever-increasing breadth of index products available, it is possible to execute an active strategy using index products.

Passive Vs. Active Investing

	Passive Investing	Active Investing
Investment Objective	Seeks to track an identified benchmark.	Seeks to outperform an identified benchmark.
Approach	Portfolio constructed via replicating an underlying index.	Portfolio constructed via security selection.
Costs	Lower management fees.	More expensive than passive funds because of higher management fees.
Investor Profile	Usually adopted by less experienced and less sophisticated investors.	Usually adopted by professional fund managers and sophisticated investors.

1.7 History of Index Investing

John Bogle, the founder of Vanguard Group, Inc. is generally accepted as the father of Index investing. In 1976, Bogle spearheaded the launching of the Vanguard 500 Index Fund, the first index fund for individual investors. His rationale for this strategy was to make investing simple and to lower the cost of investing (Chen, 2022). At that time, the concept of an index fund was met with a lot of scepticism and John Bogle's foray into index funds was termed "Bogle's folly". Suffice to say that this initiative by John Bogle gave birth to a whole new industry and ultimately led to the development of the Exchange-Traded Fund industry. The practice of index investing has grown phenomenally over the years. Some reports show that as at end of 2023, Global passive equity fund AUM was higher than global active equity fund AUM (Murugaboopathy, 2024).

1.8   Index Funds

An index fund is a type of mutual fund that seeks to track the returns of a market index (Investor.gov).

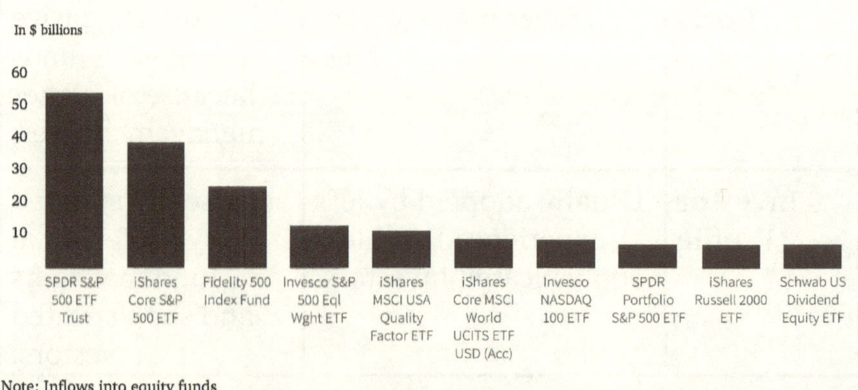

Note: Inflows into equity funds
Source: London Stock Exchange Group

Fig. 1.1: Money inflows into global passive funds in 2023

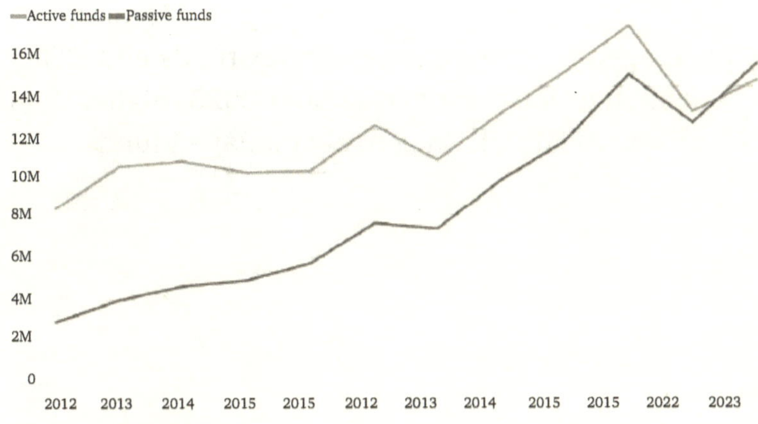

Note: Amount in $ millions
Source: London Stock Exchange Group Eikon Financial Analysis

Fig. 1.2: Global passive equity funds overtake active equity funds in net assets

Index funds are structured as mutual funds and work by replicating the composition of a specific index. With index funds, the fund manager does not select securities for inclusion in the portfolio but simply buys all the components of the relevant index in the same weighting in which they are represented in the index. Since their introduction, index funds have become quite popular for a number of reasons including but not limited to generally lower costs than traditional mutual funds and the inherent diversification characteristic of Index funds.

Also, based on their historical performance, Index funds have proven their viability as investment products. In the US for example, the active equity mutual fund AUM as a percentage of total mutual funds AUM has dramatically changed in the last few decades. In early 1990s, active mutual funds were about 97% of the total U.S. fund market but have dropped to 46%

by 2021 (Saldanha, 2024). Also, according to Morningstar, total AUM managed by passive funds (index funds and ETFs) was $13.29 trillion at the end of December 2023, higher than the $13.23 trillion AUM held in actively managed funds.

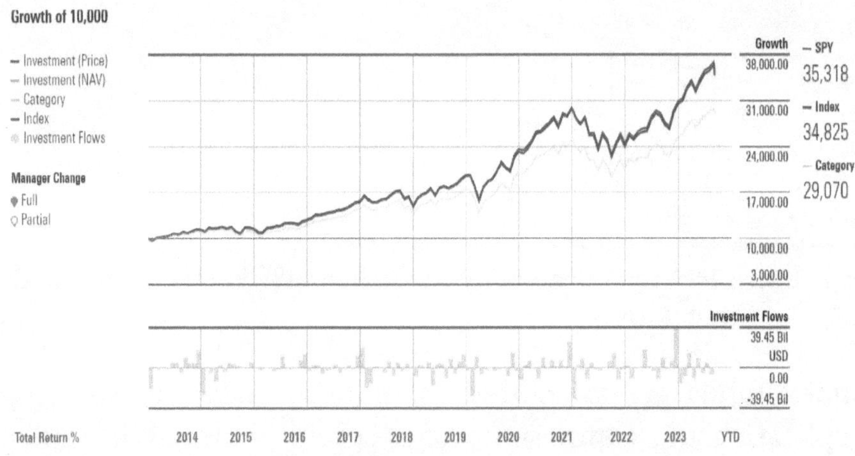

Fig. 1.3: Performance of the SPDR S&P 500 ETF

Source: *Morningstar.com*

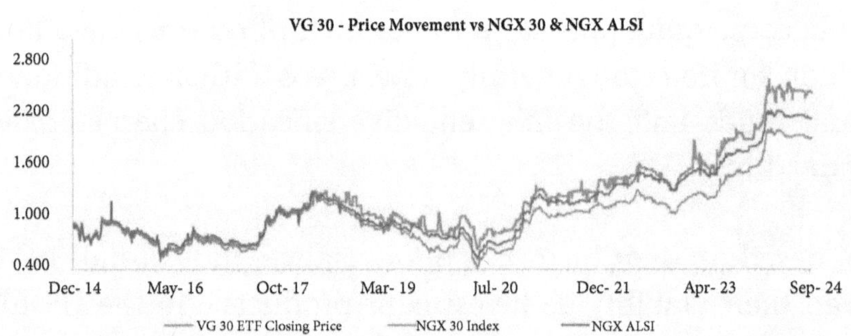

Fig. 1.4: Performance of the Vetiva Griffin 30 ETF vs NGX ALSI

Source: *Vetiva Research*

1.9   Advantages and Disadvantages of Index Funds

The following are the advantages of index investing:

- **Low cost:** An Index Fund tracks an index and as such does not involve active management of assets. Index fund management fees are therefore typically lower than those of traditional mutual funds.

- **Provides diversification:** Index funds typically invest in a basket of assets as determined by the relevant index being tracked. This helps to diversify away from asset specific risk (idiosyncratic risk).

- **Ease of ongoing management:** Index Fund managers do not need to vary portfolio allocations or track individual asset performance and thus index funds are generally easier to manage.

The following are the disadvantages of Index Investing:

- **Upside potential is restricted to the performance of the index:** In effect, an index reflects the simple average or weighted average performance of a basket of securities, hence the index return is largely restricted to an average. As such, any expected positive outlier performance from any of the index constituents cannot be fully taken advantage of (in an index fund) by taking an overweight position in the security.

- **There is no downside protection:** For example: Assuming there is negative news on one of the component companies in an index, in an active portfolio, the portfolio manager would be able to sell or underweight the stock to provide downside protection. In an index portfolio however, as long as the component stock is in the index, it would have to remain in the portfolio in the same weighting as in the benchmark index.

- **There is restricted flexibility to express investor views on the market:** For example: if a portfolio is tracking the NGX 30, the portfolio would need to replicate the weighting of the component securities in the index regardless of the view of the portfolio manager on certain stocks or sectors represented in the portfolio.

Key Takeaways

- *An index is used to track a group or basket of securities, derivatives, or other financial instruments that represent and measure the performance of a specific market, asset class, market sector, or investment strategy.*

- *In a weighted index, the constituent securities do not have the same relevance or impact on the computation of the index value. In an unweighted index, each security has the same level of relevance or impact on the index.*

- *In Africa we have the FTSE/JSE Africa All Share Index, which is a broad market index that measures the performance of stocks listed on the Johannesburg Stock Exchange and the NGX All-Share Index, which tracks the general market movement of listed equities on the Nigerian Exchange.*

- *To compute the market value of a listed company, the price of the security is multiplied by the number of units listed.*

- *To compute a price weighted index, the prices of all the component stocks is summed up and divided by a predetermined divisor.*

- *Strategic beta can be explained as any index or related investment product that seeks to provide criteria to determine the weighting of the components of an index using a strategy other than conventional market-cap weighting strategies.*

- *An index divisor is a number used to divide the total market capitalisation of an Index to arrive a predetermined Index value (called the base index value) on the date the index is launched.*

Key Takeaways

- *The NGX All-Share Index was launched in January 1984 with a base value of 100.*

- *Index investing is a portfolio management strategy in which the investor buys assets with the intention of replicating the composition of an index.*

- *Some argue that based on the efficient market hypothesis or efficient market theory, which assumes that all the information that can influence the price of an asset is available to all market participants at the same time, it is impossible to beat the market on a sustainable basis, and hence any attempts to beat the market on an ongoing basis is futile.*

- *Index funds are structured as mutual funds and work by replicating the composition of a specific index.*

- *Index fund management fees are typically lower than those of traditional mutual funds.*

Chapter 2

UNDERSTANDING EXCHANGE-TRADED FUNDS

"Don't look for the needle in the haystack. Just buy the haystack!"
– John C. Bogle, The Little Book of Common-Sense Investing: The Only
Way to Guarantee Your Fair Share of Stock Market Returns

2.1   Introduction

In the last chapter we looked at Index funds and, in this chapter, we will focus on Exchange-Traded Funds as investment products. Exchange-Traded Funds (ETFs) are very similar to index funds. The primary difference between ETFs and Index funds, however, is that Index funds can only be purchased or sold through a fund manager at the end of a trading day (this is because they are priced once a day) whilst an ETF trades like any other stock on an exchange and as such reflects a price throughout the trading day.

Let's define Exchange-Traded Funds (ETFs): ETFs are pooled-investment products listed on an Exchange which invest in a basket of securities with the objective of tracking an index or the price movement of an asset. ETFs combine some of the characteristics of mutual funds (unit trusts) with some characteristics of listed securities.

2.2   History of Exchange-Traded Funds

The world's first ETF, the Toronto 35 Index(R) Participation Fund was listed in March 1990 on the Toronto Stock Exchange (ticker symbol -"TIPs"), tracking the TSX-35 index. The ETF currently trades as the iShares S&P/TSX 60 Index ETF (Toronto Stock Exchange, 2020). The first ETF listing in the United States of America was in 1993, with the listing of an S&P 500 ETF, which tracks the S&P 500 market index. Africa's first ETF, the Satrix 40 ETF, was listed on the Johannesburg Stock Exchange in 2000. Since these initial listings, ETFs have grown both in assets under management and offering types that are available to the investing public.

ETFs have been successful for several reasons. Firstly, ETFs are relatively transparent when compared to traditional active mutual funds. The composition of an ETF portfolio is available to the public and the composition of the index being tracked is also public information. In addition, the rules guiding relevant operations of the Index e.g. rebalancing activity and performance can be tracked in line with the relevant index. Also, ETFs have typically lower cost profiles than traditional mutual funds because of lower management fees and lastly, ETFs are easier to manage as investors do not need to worry about the performance of individual security components of the ETF portfolio.

ETFs in Nigeria
The Newgold ETF
The Vetiva Griffin 30 ETF
The Greenwich Alpha ETF
The Lotus Capital Halal ETF
The Meristem Growth ETF
The Meristem Value ETF
The Stanbic ETF 30
The Stanbic ETF 40
The Vetiva Banking ETF
The Vetiva Consumer Goods ETF
The Vetiva Industrials ETF
The Vetiva S&P Nigerian Sovereign Bonds ETF

Fig. 2.1: List of ETFs in Nigeria as at 30th September 2024

2.3   Growth of the Exchange-Traded Fund Industry

In an article by Kamil Kaczmarski, Sean Farrar, and Philipp Zelter on *www.oliverwyman.com*, the authors attribute the growth in exchange-traded funds (ETFs) as the single most disruptive trend within the asset management industry over the last 20 years (Kamil Kaczmarski). In the past 5 years, Global Exchange-Traded Fund (ETF) assets under management ("AUM") has grown by a Compound Annual Growth Rate ("CAGR") of 18.9%, and has grown by more than 25% from December 2022 to reach a new record of almost $11.5 trillion at the end of 2023 according to a report published by PWC titled - ETFs 2028: Shaping the future.

According to experts, there are a number of factors that are likely to further drive the growth of the ETF industry into the future. A key factor is that investors are becoming increasingly sensitive to costs and ETFs present a low-cost investment vehicle. Also, the increase in the sophistication and nature of ETFs available to investors have made it easier for ETFs to be used to pursue active strategies.

2.4   Features of Exchange-Traded Funds

- A key difference between ETFs and mutual funds is that ETFs can trade on an intra-day basis on an exchange, like any other stock, whilst mutual funds are bought or sold at end of the trading day.

- ETFs are passive investment vehicles and ETF portfolios track a benchmark such as an index or the price of an asset. Most mutual funds, except index funds, are actively managed.

- ETFs are typically low-cost investment vehicles and have lower expense ratios than traditional mutual funds.

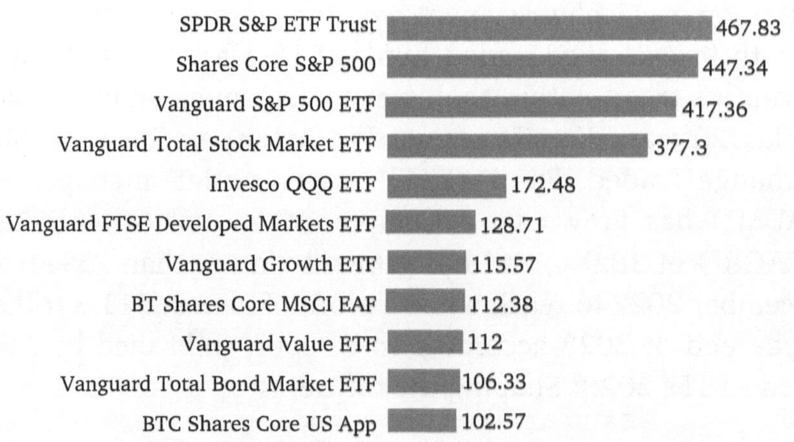

Fig. 2.2:   Market capitalization of largest Exchange-Traded funds (ETFs) worldwide as of March 2024 (in billion U.S. dollars).

Source: *(Statistica)*

2.5   Types of Exchange-Traded Funds

There are very many different types of ETFs. This is because an ETF can be constructed theoretically on any index or asset type. To drill down into the various types of ETFs that are available, we can make use of the following categories: Classification by Asset Class, Classification by Structure, and Classification by Strategy or Focus.

2.5.1 Classification by Asset Class

- **Equity ETFs:** These are the most common type of ETFs currently available. Equity ETFs track equity indices such as the S&P 500 Index, the NGX All-Share Index, or the Ghana Stock Exchange Composite Index.

- **Fixed Income (Bond) ETFs:** Fixed income ETFs have the benefit of giving investors access to fixed income securities, some of which are not readily accessible to retail investors. Fixed Income ETFs are also useful for investors who desire current income and can also be used to diversify an equity portfolio. Underlying assets can be sovereign bonds or corporate bonds.

- **Commodity ETFs:** Commodity ETFs are used to provide exposure to a specific commodity or several commodities e.g., precious metals, agricultural commodities. The underlying assets of commodity ETFs can be the physical commodity or futures contracts.

  Many commodity exchange traded products (ETPs) are structured as Exchange-Traded Notes (ETNs) and not Exchange-Traded Funds. ETNs are debt securities issued by a financial institution with an obligation to deliver the return of an index or asset price.

Managing commodity ETPs which hold futures contracts, can be a bit complicated as there are risks associated with "contango" and "backwardation". Contango is when the forward price of a futures contract is higher than its spot price. On the other hand, Backwardation is when the forward price of a futures contract is lower than the spot price.

Why is this relevant? Unlike equities or physical commodities that can be held for as long as necessary or as required, futures contract expire and must be replaced in the ETF Portfolio to maintain the relevant index exposure. Therefore, an ETF holding futures contracts would have to "roll" into another futures contract as the current one expires. Therefore, in a contango scenario, the ETF return is negatively impacted, and vice versa in a backwardation scenario.

Example: For a hypothetical ETF called the "Nigeria Brent Crude Futures ETF", let's assume that the ETF is invested in crude oil futures contracts worth $50/barrel. Towards expiration of the contract, to ensure that the ETF continues to hold relevant underlying assets, the fund Manager purchases another contract at the price of $100/barrel for maturity at a later date, resulting in a 50% loss for the ETF investors. It is important to note that a reverse scenario is also possible i.e., a backwardation scenario in which the contract purchased for maturity at a future date is at the price of $30/barrel, for example, resulting in a gain for the ETF investors.

- **Currency ETFs:** Currency ETFs provide investors exposure to a single currency or a basket of currencies. Currency ETFs can be used to diversify currency risk or can also be used to speculate and trade on currencies. Some currency ETFs hold the actual underlying currency whilst others use derivative products. By the nature of the underlying asset, currency ETF returns are usually based on capital appreciation as currency ETF distributions are limited, if any, (Nasdaq, 2023).

- **Real Estate ETFs:** Real Estate ETFs invest mainly in Real Estate Investment Trusts (REITS). REITS can be structured as investment companies or unit trusts. There are different types of REITS, which include but are not limited to Equity REITs and Mortgage REITs. Equity REITs invest in physical Real Estate Assets whilst Mortgage REITs invest in mortgage debt.

2.5.2   Classification by Structure

- **Physical ETFs:** These are the most common types of ETFs. Physical ETFs achieve index replication by holding the actual underlying assets represented in the index. For example, an Equity ETF can hold the actual shares in the index under a Trust structure to back the ETF units. Physical ETFs are regarded as relatively safe structures with little or no credit risk involved.

  Physical ETFs can either be fully replicated or optimised. In a fully replicated ETF, the ETF holds all the securities or assets in the index in the exact weightings or composition of the index. In an **optimised ETF**, the fund holds securities that can represent the excluded components of the index whilst preserving the nature of the index. This can be achieved through a process called sampling or optimised sampling. An example is the Russell 2000 Index which tracks the performance of 2,000 small-cap U.S. equities. To track this index, an ETF may not be able to hold all the 2,000 stocks but may use a sampling strategy to replicate the index.

- **Synthetic ETF:** Synthetic ETFs do not invest in the actual underlying assets but in relevant derivatives. Synthetic ETFs are common in Commodity ETFs e.g. Crude Oil or Precious Metal ETFs.

2.5.3   Classification by Strategy or Focus

These ETFs are focused on providing investor exposure to specific market segments, themes, strategies, or sectors. Examples are:

- **Thematic ETFs:** As the name suggests, Thematic ETFs are exchange-traded funds that seek to provide investor exposure to specific trends, or themes e.g., Artificial intelligence, sustainability, etc. They provide an investment vehicle for investors to express their interests or strategies.

  Thematic ETFs are different from Sector ETFs because whilst sector ETFs focus on a single sector or industry, themes can cut across industries e.g. ESG themes (Jark, 2024).

  An example of a thematic ETF would be the Global X U.S. Infrastructure Development ETF PAVE with over $7billion in assets (*www.etf.com*). The ETF seeks to invest in companies that stand to benefit from a potential increase in infrastructure activity in the United States, including those involved in the production of raw materials, heavy equipment, engineering, and construction (*www.globalxetfs.com*). To take advantage of emerging opportunities, thematic ETFs focus on forward-looking opportunities, e.g., in technology (Blackrock Advisor Centre).

- **Leveraged ETFs:** Leveraged ETFs seek to magnify the return of the index which they track (Carlson, 2024). It is important to note that leveraged ETFs do not invest directly in the underlying assets of the index but in derivatives instruments (a contract between two or more parties that derive its value from the price of an underlying asset) with the aim of magnifying portfolio returns over and above the performance of the index they track. The use of derivatives for ETFs exposes the investor to generally higher levels of risk.

  An example of a leveraged ETF is the ProShares UltraPro QQQ. This ETF is one of the most popular and liquid leveraged ETFs. The fund seeks to deliver three times the return of the daily performance of the NASDAQ-100 Index (Killa, 2024).

- **Inverse ETFs:** Inverse ETFs are also known as "short or bear ETFs". They seek to return the opposite of the benchmark index performance and do this by investing in derivative instruments which will profit from a decline in the value of an underlying benchmark. This is similar to holding a short position on an index.

An example of an inverse ETF is the ProShares UltraPro Short QQQ (SQQQ). This ETF also uses a leverage strategy and seeks to inversely mirror the returns of the S&P 500 threefold (SALVUCCI, Updated 2022). Jeremy Salvucci in the article *"What Is an Inverse ETF? Definition, Purpose & Examples"* cites an instance on August 26, 2022, when the S&P 500 lost 3.37%, and the ProShares UltraPro Short QQQ fund went up 11.9%.

- **Smart Beta ETFs:** Smart Beta ETFs employ a set of rules of criteria e.g. earnings, liquidity, and dividends to determine the composition of the ETF portfolio (Corporate Finance Institute). These ETFs are known to combine both passive and active strategies in one ETF product.

2.6   Emerging ETF Trends

According to the PwC report titled, "ETFs 2028: shaping the future", even though ETFs tracking traditional assets classes i.e., equities and fixed income remain dominant within the ETF space, innovation within the ETF industry has resulted in a growing list of diversified ETF products. For example, after many years of lobbying, the US SEC approved the first physical bitcoin ETFs in January 2024. Also, in April 2024, the Securities and Futures Commission (SFC) of Hong Kong approved spot ETFs for Bitcoin and Ethereum.

Further to the above, Active ETFs are one of the ETF products that many analysts believe may catalyse the growth of the Global ETF industry.

What are Active ETFs? In contrast with traditional exchange-traded funds which track indices, an active exchange-traded fund (Active ETF) has component securities and weightings determined by a Portfolio Manager (Reiff, 2024). Also, while traditional ETFs seek to replicate the performance of a benchmark, active ETFs seek to outperform a benchmark. Active ETFs seek to take advantage of the benefits of active management and the benefits inherent in exchange-traded funds as products. An obvious advantage of active ETFs is that they can potentially deliver returns that are higher than market returns. By implication as well, Active ETFs carry more risk and are not as transparent as traditional ETFs which trade indices. An example of an Active ETF is the Fidelity Magellan ETF (FMAG).

Key Takeaways

- *ETFs are pooled-investment products listed on an Exchange which invest in a basket of securities with the objective of tracking an index or the price movement of an asset.*

- *A key difference between ETFs and Mutual Funds is that ETFs can trade on an intra-day basis, like any other stock, whilst mutual funds are bought or sold at end of the trading day.*

- *ETFs can be classified by Asset Class, structure and by strategy or focus.*

- *Contango is when the forward price of a futures contract is higher than its spot price. On the other hand, Backwardation is when the forward price of a futures contract is lower than the spot price.*

- *In an optimised ETF, the fund holds securities that can represent the excluded components of the index whilst preserving the nature of the index.*

- *Leveraged ETFs seek to magnify the return of the index which they track.*

- *One of the ETF products which many analysts believe may catalyse the growth of the Global ETF industry are Active ETFs.*

<h1 style="text-align:center">Chapter 3</h1>

EXCHANGE-TRADED FUNDS AND PORTFOLIO CONSTRUCTION

Predicting rain doesn't count. Building arks does. – Warren Buffett

3.1 Introduction

An optimal portfolio is a portfolio that is exposed to the minimum level of risk for the desired level of return. In this chapter, we will be looking at the various ways in which Exchange-Traded Funds can support the construction of optimal portfolios. Exchange-Traded Funds can be powerful investment tools in constructing portfolios that can be used to achieve portfolio allocation objectives and execute various Portfolio strategies.

3.2 Portfolio Construction Objectives

The first step in Portfolio Construction is to have an investment objective that reflects the specific circumstances, aspirations, goals, and objectives of the investor. Some of the possible portfolio objectives are:

- **Capital Preservation:** This is the objective of safeguarding, protecting, and preserving the initial value of an investment. To achieve this, the investor will need to adopt a conservative approach to the management of the portfolio to minimize the risk the portfolio is exposed to. This approach or strategy also influences the nature of investments that can be utilized in the portfolio. Securities that are suitable for conservative portfolios usually have a short-term profile and the issuer should have the highest credit profile possible e.g., government backed securities or treasuries.

- **Current income:** this is the objective of seeking investment securities that will provide the maximum level of distributions or cash return for the portfolio. This can be achieved by a focus on high dividend yield stocks, money market instruments, government or corporate bonds, or annuity products.

- **Aggressive growth:** This objective focuses on making the highest returns possible in the shortest possible time. An aggressive growth objective comes with some risk as the type of securities that can deliver aggressive growth are typically risker. Portfolios with an aggressive growth objective usually have a very high allocation to equities and also within the equities asset class, such portfolios usually target growth stocks.

- **Balanced growth:** This strategy focuses on diversifying a portfolio across asset classes and across various categories within each asset class. This serves to lower the risk of the portfolio whilst targeting moderate returns on the portfolio.

3.3 Portfolio Risk

All investment portfolios carry some level of risk and from an investment portfolio perspective, risk can be defined as the possibility that the actual portfolio return will be different from the expected portfolio return.

In constructing a portfolio, it is important to understand and reflect the risk profile or risk tolerance of the investor. The risk tolerance of an investor is the amount of capital loss the investor is willing to bear in the process of seeking returns. From a risk point of view, investors are usually profiled as being aggressive, moderate, or conservative and an investor's risk profile is usually influenced by some factors including but not limited to the age of the investor, the financial circumstance of the investor and the specific objective of the investment portfolio.

Why is an understanding of the risk tolerance of an investor important? It influences the portfolio asset allocation decision that is taken on the portfolio i.e. the weightings that are apportioned to various asset classes or security types.

It is important to understand that there is relationship between risk and return. The higher the level of risk a portfolio is exposed to, the higher the level of potential return that is expected from the Portfolio. Two major types of risk are relevant to all Portfolios:

- **Systematic Risk:** This is known as market risk. These are risks that are relevant to the whole market and as such cannot be managed through diversification. Examples of systematic risks are political risk, inflation risk, interest rate risk, etc.

- **Unsystematic Risk:** This is also known as specific risk or idiosyncratic risk. This risk is specific to an asset, security, industry, or market segment. The key strategy to manage unsystematic risk is portfolio diversification.

Measuring Risk: There are some methods used to measure risk in a portfolio. These include, but are not limited to, computation of the standard deviation of a portfolio, the Portfolio Beta and the Sharpe ratio of the Portfolio.

- **The Standard Deviation** of a Portfolio in essence measures the volatility of a portfolio around its mean.

- **The Portfolio Beta** measures the returns or performance of a Portfolio relative to the broad market.

- **The Sharpe Ratio** measures the risk adjusted returns of a portfolio. There is an inverse relationship between the standard deviation and sharpe ratio of a portfolio.

Worked Example: Computation of Sharpe Ratio

Sharpe Ratio = (Rp − Rf) ÷ σp

Where:

Rp = Expected Portfolio Return

Rf = Risk-Free Rate

σp = Standard Deviation of Portfolio (Risk)

Question: Portfolio A has an expected return of 5.0% and a standard deviation of 6.0%. What is the Sharpe ratio? (Assume risk free rate is 2.5%)

Expected Portfolio Return (Rp) = 5.0%

Risk-Free Rate (Rf) = 2.5%

Standard Deviation of Portfolio (σp) = 6.0%

Sharpe Ratio = (5.0% – 2.5%) ÷ 6.0% = 0.41x

Interpreting Sharp Ratio

It is generally accepted that:

Sharpe Ratio < 1.0x → suboptimal, Portfolio Return
Sharpe Ratio > 1.0x → Acceptable Portfolio Return
Sharpe Ratio > 2.0x → Strong Portfolio Return
Sharpe Ratio > 3.0x → Excellent

3.4 Use of ETFs in Asset Allocation

In the portfolio construction process, after identifying the objective of the portfolio and assessing the risk profile of the investor, the focus needs to be on the allocation strategy (i.e., the method of apportioning portfolio assets in line with desired objectives). Whilst allocation considerations are critically important, there is no "one size fits all" allocation. Investor decisions are influenced by many factors and as such, portfolio allocations are unique to each investor. Suffice to say, the allocation decision is arguably the most important decision for the investor when building a portfolio.

It should be noted that Portfolio allocation decisions are critical to the ultimate performance of portfolios and involve the amount of portfolio funds that are allocated to different asset classes e.g., equities, fixed income, cash and money market instruments, and alternative assets. Portfolio allocation also involves the selection of securities that are within each asset class. *So then, how can we apportion assets in a portfolio, also including ETFs?* At the asset class level, one way to approach this is to look at the various alternative asset classes or categories of investments available, and based on the prognosis/outlook of each asset class, ETFs that provide exposure to those asset classes can be used, in full or partially in addition to security selection, to achieve desired asset class weightings. A similar process is also deployed at the sub-asset class level for the purpose of fulfilling sector or industry weightings etc. ETFs can also be used to fulfill allocation obligation to asset classes or specific assets/securities that may be difficult to access e.g., Gold.

3.5   Use of ETFs to Achieve Diversification

Because most ETFs in themselves carry a diversification benefit, ETFs can be used to diversify an existing portfolio.

Example: Investor A has a global portfolio valued at ₦1,000,000.00 (One Million Naira) which is invested only in Government Bonds. After a recent review of the portfolio, Investor A wishes to introduce equities exposure to the portfolio to optimize its risk-return profile. One of the ways Investor A can achieve this, through the use of an ETF, is to liquidate a portion of the current portfolio and invest the proceeds in a broad market equity ETF.

What has investor A achieved? Without having to go through the rigour of selecting specific equities, Investor A has been able to: 1) Diversify the Portfolio by having both equities and fixed income components of the portfolio; and 2) Within the equities asset class, investor A has achieved diversification because the broad market equity ETF exposes the portfolio to a basket of equities that reflect the market.

3.6 Use of ETFs to Rebalance a Portfolio

The objective of rebalancing a portfolio is to maintain a target allocation through the selling and buying of securities that have become overweight or underweight through price movements. This is important because changes in the prices of the component securities of a portfolio may cause the portfolio to deviate from its intended asset allocation.

Worked Example: A hypothetical equity portfolio has an intended portfolio allocation of 60% to Sector A (comprised of two companies C & D) and 40% to Sector B (comprised of two companies E & F). At Inception of the portfolio, the portfolio is structured as shown below:

Portfolio as a 31st May, 2024

Stock	No. of Units (million)	Market Price ₦	Market Value (₦ million)	Sector Weighting (%)
Company C	1	20.00	20.00	
Company D	4	10.00	40.00	
Sector A Total			**60.00**	60%

Stock	No of Units	Market Price	Market Value	Sector Weighting
Company E	1	15.00	15.00	
Company F	5	5.00	25.00	
Sector B Total			**40.00**	40%
TOTAL PORTFOLIO			**100.00**	100%

Over one month, based on movement in the prices of the component securities of the two sectors, the market value of Sector A has lost ₦40million, and the market value of Sector B has gained ₦40million. Based on this, the portfolio looked like the below on the 30th of June 2024 (note that there has been no purchase or sale of securities):

Stock	No of Units	Market Price (31st May) ₦	Market Price (30th June) ₦	Market Value – 30th June (₦'million)	Sector Weighting (%)
Company C	1	20.00	10.00	10.00	
Company D	4	10.00	2.50	10.00	
Sector A Total				**20.00**	20%
Company E	1	15.00	30.00	30.00	
Company F	5	5.00	10.00	50.00	
Sector B Total				80.00	80%
TOTAL PORTFOLIO				100.00	100%

As we can see from the above, there has been a significant deviation from the intended portfolio allocation based solely on the movement of security prices within Sectors A and B. The above scenario can trigger the need to rebalance the portfolio to ensure the intended portfolio allocation is maintained.

Question: Using the above example, with the use of ETFs, how can the portfolio manager rebalance the portfolio to maintain a 60% allocation to Sector A and a 40% allocation to Sector B.

Step 1: Sell securities in Sector B worth ₦40m to create a cash position. This can be achieved by selling 4 units of Company F at the market price of ₦10.00.

Stock	No of Units	Market Price (30th June) ₦	Market Value – 30th June (N 'million)	Sector Weighting (%)
Company C	1	10.00	10.00	
Company D	4	2.50	10.00	
Sector A Total			**20.00**	20%
Company E	1	30.00	30.00	
Company F	1	10.00	10.00	
Sector B Total			**40.00**	40%
Cash from sale of company F			**40.00**	40%
TOTAL PORTFOLIO			**100.00**	100%

Step 2: Use the cash position to purchase an ETF that gives exposure to Sector A:

Stock	No of Units	Market Price (30th June) ₦	Market Value – 30th June (₦ million)	Sector Weighting (%)
Company C	1	10.00	10.00	
Company D	4	2.50	10.00	
Sector A - ETF			40.00	
Sector A Total			**60.00**	60%
Company E	1	30.00	30.00	
Company F	1	10.00	10.00	
Sector B Total			**40.00**	40%
TOTAL PORTFOLIO			**100.00**	100%

3.7   ETF-only Portfolios

In the previous sections, we have looked at how ETFs can be used alongside other securities in portfolio construction, and we have also looked at how ETFs can be used to rebalance portfolios. In this section, we will look at how to build ETF-only portfolios to express different portfolio allocation objectives.

To achieve this, let's use a hypothetical equity portfolio called "Mercury". Building an Equity portfolio with ETFs follows the same principles as building any portfolio. The first step is to have an investment objective. For Portfolio Mercury, let's have an objective of outperforming the general market, i.e., the NGX All-Share Index. To achieve this, as with any other investment objective, the focus needs to be on the allocation strategy.

So then, how can we apportion assets of Portfolio Mercury in an all-equity ETF portfolio? One way to approach this is using ETFs to achieve sector exposure / desired sector weightings. A variation of this is using a core-satellite strategy. What does this mean? This involves having the main portion of a portfolio in a broad market ETF to provide stability to the portfolio and then having other peripheral investments or "satellites" by picking ETFs that reflect market segments or assets that are expected to outperform and deliver superior returns.

For example, using the core-satellite approach, one can start with a core (main) diversified exposure (say 40% - 70%) to the general market using an ETF that seeks to give exposure to the whole market (e.g., the NGX All-share index or NGX-30 index). Following this, a selection of sector-specific ETFs can then be introduced to give exposure to sectors that are expected to deliver superior returns. Let's look at a hypothetical scenario in which the view is that the Banking Sector will outperform other sectors in 2025, in constructing a Portfolio, one could consider allocating more funds to a Banking Sector ETF (e.g., another 20% in addition to the core ETF allocation), with supporting positions in other sectors with positive prognosis.

In our example above, a sample/dummy Equity ETF portfolio could look like this:

Broad Equity Market ETF – 60%, Banking Sector ETF – 20%, Industrials Sector ETF – 10%, Consumer Good sector ETF – 10% (please note that this is a dummy portfolio and should not be implemented).

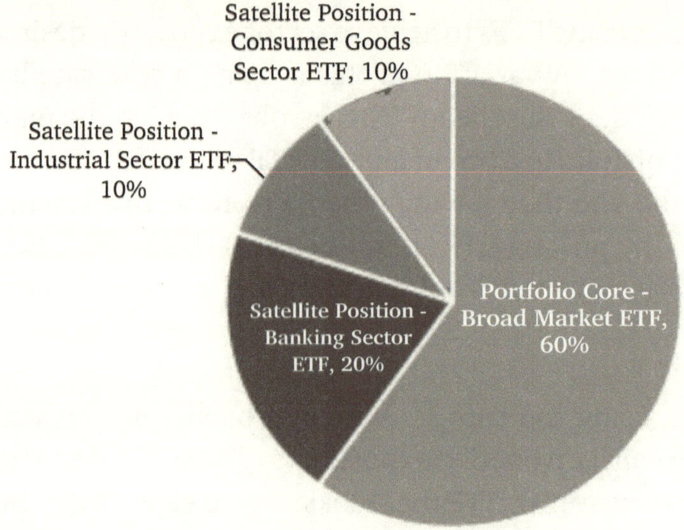

Fig. 3:1   Portfolio Construction using ETFs

One can further drill down to the effective sector allocation of this dummy portfolio by looking at the weightings of sector components of the core segment of the Portfolio and adding same to the additional sector weightings achieved via the sector ETFs, to give a picture of the global sector weightings. With this information, allocations can be tweaked, at the core or satellite component level, to achieve an optimal Portfolio allocation.

Effective Allocation of the Portfolio

Sector	Broad Market ETF Adjusted Sector weighting	Sector ETF weighting	***Effective Weight
Banking	13.92% x 60% = 8.35%	20%	28.35%
Industrials	27.64% x 60% = 16.58%	10%	26.58%
Consumer Goods	17.22% x 60% = 10.33%	10%	23.33%
Others	41.22 x 60% = 24.73%		24.73%

*** *rounding off errors exist.*

Even though the weighting of the banking sector in the broad market ETF is 13.92%. We have been able to achieve an effective portfolio allocation of 28.35% by restricting the allocation of the broad market index to 60% and including a 20% satellite allocation to a banking ETF.

Key Takeaways

- *The first step in Portfolio Construction is to have an investment objective that reflects the specific circumstances, aspirations, goals, and objectives of the investor.*

- *Systematic Risks are risks that are relevant to the whole market and as such cannot be readily mitigated through diversification. Examples of systematic risks are political risk, inflation risk, interest rate risk etc.*

- *An allocation decision is arguably the most important decision for the investor when building a portfolio.*

- *The objective of rebalancing a portfolio is to maintain a target allocation through selling and buying securities that have become overweight or underweight through price movements.*

- *Changes in the prices of the component securities of a portfolio may cause the portfolio to deviate from its intended asset allocation thereby requiring rebalancing.*

- *Idiosyncratic risks are specific to an asset, security, industry or market segment. The key strategy to mitigate Idiosyncratic risk is portfolio diversification.*

- *Building an Equity portfolio with ETFs follows the same principles as building any portfolio. The first step is to have an investment objective.*

- *In core and satellite investing, the majority of portfolio is invested in a passive fund as the portfolio's core. The rest of the portfolio is then invested using active strategies (the satellites).*

Chapter 4

STRUCTURING AN EXCHANGE-TRADED FUND

"There shall be an ETF for every asset class, and it shall be virtually free to own." – Matt Hougan & Dave Nadig via ETF.com

4.1   Introduction

In this chapter, we will discuss some important steps and considerations in structuring an ETF for listing on an Exchange. It is important to note that the structure of a proposed ETF is influenced by the regulatory environment in which the ETF will be listed. Kindly note that where there is a conflict between any representation in this book and relevant regulation, the regulation supersedes.

4.2   ETFs Structures

ETFs can take a variety of structures but are most commonly structured as open-ended funds. This means that they can take on new investors after an initial listing and additional ETF units can be created. In Nigeria, all ETFs are required to be registered with the Securities and Exchange Commission and listed on a recognised Exchange, e.g. the NGX. Also, there are rules and regulations issued by the SEC and the NGX guiding the operations of ETFs in Nigeria. The objective of the rules is to ensure transparency (i.e., that investors have adequate information to make investment decisions) and to ensure investment risks are minimized. Please see below the NGX requirements in respect of the listing of ETFs in Nigeria.

ETFs shall:
- *be open-ended, unless otherwise approved.*

- *be issued over an index (and disclose the methodology of computation of the index) or be structured on any one or a combination of equities; commodities; currency inflation rate, or financial instruments based on a given ratio acceptable to The Exchange.*

- *disclose the methodology of computation of the NAV of ETF.*

- *be fully backed at all times; either by an acquisition of the underlying equities, commodities, assets, or financial instruments it represents, and proxy securities acceptable to NGX which should be listed, freely tradable and have adequate liquidity or cash.*

- *hold Portfolio Assets which shall be held by a trust or in custody with a third party (unrelated to the sponsor or originator of the ETF) and a trustee or custodian shall be appointed, subject to approval by The Exchange, to protect the interests of the investors in the ETF.*

(source: NGX)

4.3 The ETF Ecosystem

Now that we have a general understanding of the structure for ETFs in Nigeria, let's look at some of the parties that are relevant to the functioning of an ETF.

- **ETF Sponsor:** This is the entity that is the issuer of the ETF and has overall responsibility for the listing of the ETF.

- **Fund Manager:** The fund manager of an ETF is responsible for managing the underlying assets of an ETF and ensures that the underlying assets track the desired benchmark. For this role, the fund manager is paid a Management Fee.

- **Authorised Dealer (AD):** Also known as the authorised participant. The AD is a Primary Market player and is responsible for ensuring continued liquidity for the ETF through the creation and redemption process and acts as a Wholesaler of the ETF units. The AD role is critical because it provides liquidity to the ETF and facilitates efficient price discovery. The Authorized Dealer should have the financial capacity and the willingness to keep an inventory of the ETF units and the underlying Assets.

- **ETF Market Maker:** The Market maker is a Securities Dealing firm appointed by the ETF Issuer / Sponsor to ensure that the ETF units are liquid in the secondary market by being a "ready counterparty" to both buyers and sellers of the ETF units on an exchange. The key difference between an Authorised Dealer and a Market Maker is that the Authorised Dealer is a primary market participant whilst the market maker is a secondary market participant. Also, the market maker only trades the ETF units on an exchange whist the Authorised Dealer deals in both the ETF units and the underlying assets in wholesale volumes. Even though both roles are distinct, the Authorized Dealer can also be, and usually is, the Market Maker for the ETF units.

- **ETF Trustee:** The ETF trustee's role is to ensure that the ETF is managed for the benefit and in the best interest of the ETF unit holders. The ETF trustee commonly holds legal title to the underlying assets of the ETF to ensure that the ETF units being held by investors are "backed up" by actual assets whose value is reflected in the pricing of the ETF units.

- **ETF Custodian:** The custodian is a bank that holds the assets of the ETF on behalf of the ETF trust.

The following highlights the relationships between the various ecosystem parties.

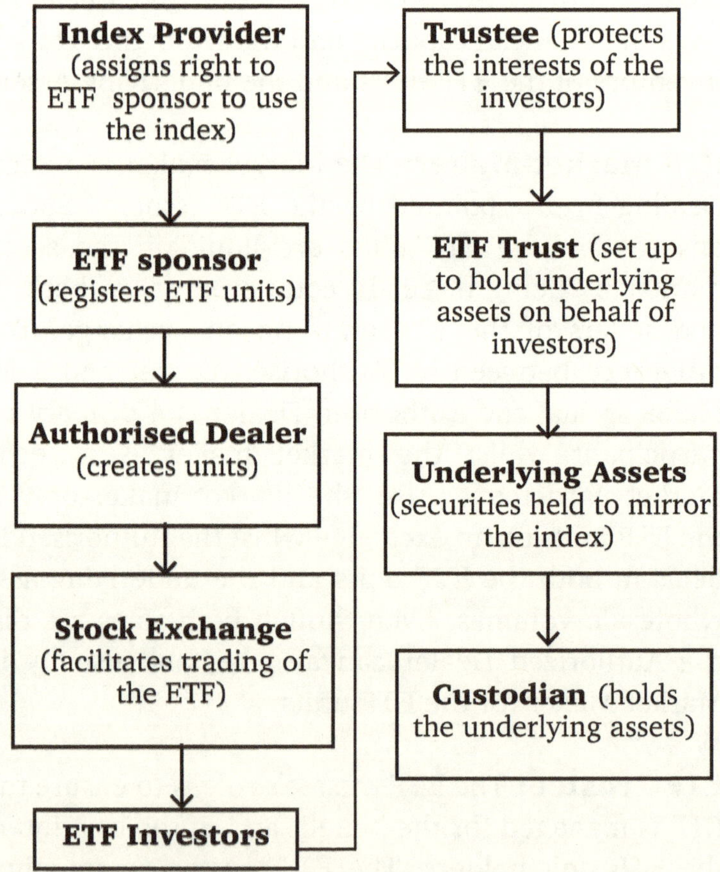

Fig. 4.1: The ETF Ecosystem

4.4   Choosing an Index

ETFs seek to replicate the performance of an index and choosing a benchmark index is therefore an important activity for an ETF issuer as it determines the basis for the ETF portfolio composition. First and foremost, the index needs to provide the appropriate exposure for the target investor e.g if an ETF sponsor wants to create an ETF that provides exposure to the broad Ghanaian equities market, an index that provides the best representation of the Ghanaian equities market should be chosen.

What if there are multiple indices that provide the same exposure? How does an ETF sponsor identify the most appropriate index to use?

Please see below relevant criteria to assess an index to be used for creating an ETF:

1. **Diversification:** Is the Index diversified? If an index has concentrated holdings, then asset or security specific risk comes to play.

2. **Is the index investible?** How easy is it to replicate the index? Are the component securities sufficiently liquid?

3. **Transparency.** Are the index rules and index construction methodology transparent?

4. **Index fees:** How high are the fees compared to alternative index products?

5. **Index rules** e.g. do you have frequent rebalancing?

4.5 **The ETF Listing Process** (please refer to relevant SEC rules or NGX regulation for the listing process)

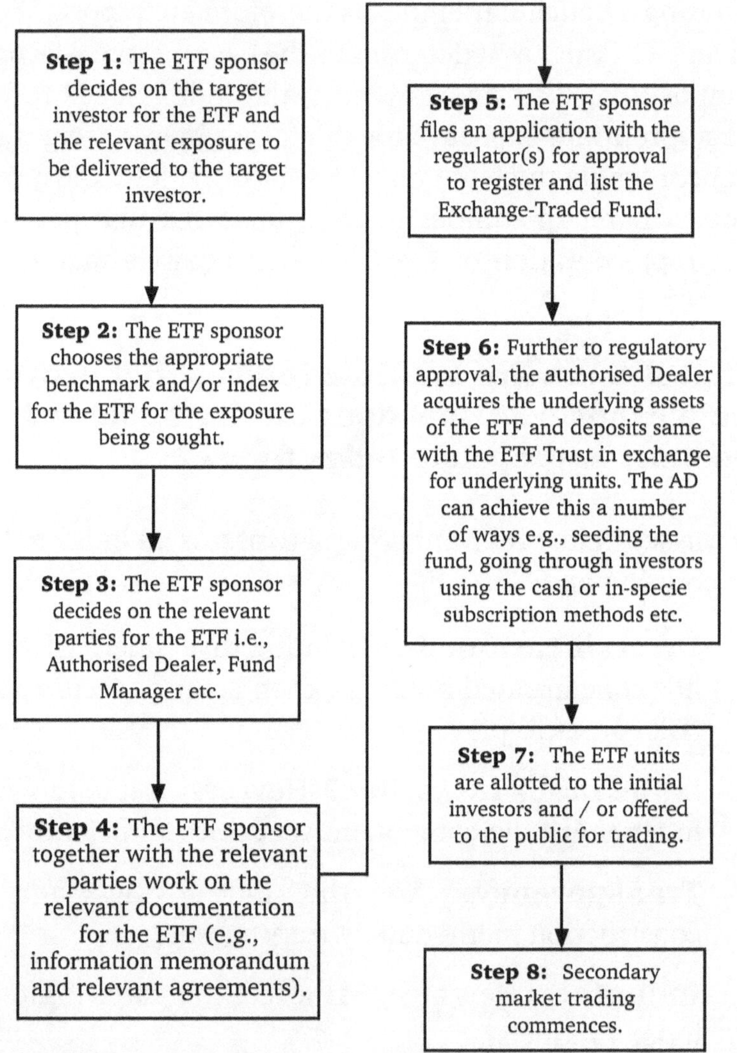

4.6   **Index Licensing**

As we have already established, ETFs are built to track or replicate the performance of indices. There are companies in the business of constructing indices. Index construction involves designing the structure of the index, defining the rules that establish eligibility criteria for securities that will be included in the index, and calculating/publishing the index values. Examples of global index providers are S&P Dow Jones Indices, MSCI, FTSE Russell, and Bloomberg. Locally, we also have the NGX, FMDQ, LCFE, NASD as index providers amongst others. ETF index licensing fees are the fees payable to index providers for the use of their indices in creating products e.g. an index fund or ETF. Index licensing fees are important because they feed into the expense ratio of an ETF. Index licensing fees usually have a fixed and variable component. The variable component is usually based on the AUM of the ETF.

4.7   Choosing an Authorised Dealer/Market Maker

From the perspective of an issuer, one of the critical parties to the successful operations of an Exchange Traded Fund is the Authorized Dealer. In Nigeria, the Authorized Dealer is a broker dealer registered with the Securities and Exchange Commission and who is a member of a securities exchange and is appointed (one or more) by the fund manager to execute the sale and purchase of ETF units with retail investors (Consolidated SEC rules, 2013). These are firms appointed by an ETF issuer to create or redeem ETF shares and act as Wholesalers of the ETF units. In choosing an Authorised Dealer, the ETF issuer should check the financial capacity of the firm to carry out the creation and redemption of the ETF units at a level that aligns with the objectives of the ETF. Also, the ETF issuer should assess the operations of the Authorised Dealer for efficiency. The Authorised Dealer and the ETF Issuer execute what is called an Authorised Dealer Agreement which gives the Authorised Dealer permission to create and redeem ETF units. Authorised Dealers sometimes deal on their own books or on behalf of institutional investors. They reduce the operational risk profile of ETFs by ensuring efficient trading and pricing of ETF units.

4.8   Creation and Redemption of ETFs

Creation is the process of sourcing the underlying assets of an ETF as a basis for the creation of additional ETF units whilst ETF redemption is the process of cancelling units of an ETF in exchange for the underlying assets.

To fully understand the Creation and Redemption process, it is important to understand the meaning of an ETF Basket. An ETF basket can be defined as the smallest viable portfolio composed of the securities that are in the index being tracked by an exchange-traded fund in the same weightings and composition as in the relevant index. **Creation Units (sometimes called ETF block)** are determined by the Authorized Dealer and refer to the minimum number of ETF baskets that can be created or redeemed by the Authorized Dealer in a single transaction. An ETF Block can be equal to, or a multiple of, the ETF basket.

Worked Example

We have an index called the "hypothetical Index" or HI Index and we want to build an Exchange-Traded Fund on the Index to be called the HI ETF. The index has two component securities: Share A that is ₦3.50 per unit and Share B that is N3.00 per unit and weightings in the Index of Share A is 70% and Share B is 30%. To ensure Retail adoption we have decided that each ETF unit should be listed at ₦1. How many ETF units make an HI ETF Basket?

Computation:

The Minimum Portfolio to replicate the index and maintain index weighting (i.e. ETF basket) is:

Stock A – 2 units at ₦3.50/unit - ₦7.00 - weighting 70%

Stock B - 1 unit at ₦3.00 /unit - ₦3.00 - weighting 30%

Minimum Portfolio Value to create a basket is -   ₦10.00

If each unit of the ETF is to be priced at ₦1, then the minimum ETF basket size will have 10 units of the ETF. Then the Creation Units Size, which we call the Block, can be equal to the basket or any multiple of 10 units depending on other considerations.

If the creation unit size is taken as 100 ETF units or 10 baskets, the creation units value will be:

Stock A – 20 units at ₦3.50/unit – ₦70.00 - weighting 70%

Stock B - 10 units at ₦3.00 /unit - ₦30.00 - weighting 30%

Block Size (creation units value):   ₦100.00

ETF Creation Process

1. ETF Fund Manager or Market Maker sends a creation request to the Authorised Dealer. The reason for this can be a need for inventory to fulfil demand for the ETF units by an investor.

2. The Authorised Dealer (Authorised Participant) purchases the relevant basket of securities or receives same from the investor wishing to subscribe.

3.   The Authorised Participant / Dealer delivers the basket of securities to the ETF Trust.

4.   Additional ETF units are created, registered / listed following relevant regulatory approvals, as necessary.

5.   ETF units are sold to or delivered to the investor.

ETF Redemption Process

1.   The Fund Manager or Market Maker issues a redemption request. The reason for this can be to remove excess inventory being held by the market maker or to execute a redemption instruction from a large investor who wishes to take custody of the underlying assets.

2.   The Authorised Dealer submits the relevant units to the fund from its own inventory or for an investor.

3.   The fund delivers the relevant basket of securities to the Authorised Dealer or investor.

4.   The ETF units submitted are cancelled.

4.9   Cash Creation vs In-specie Creation

Whilst the key transaction activity in the secondary market for ETFs is the trading of Exchange-Traded Fund units on the floors of an Exchange, in the primary market, the key transaction activity is the creation and redemption process.

Institutional investors may wish to invest in an ETF, during a primary market offering of the ETF and consideration to be exchanged by the Institutional investor for the ETF units can either be cash (cash creation) or by relinquishing the underlying securities that represent the number of units required (In-specie creation).

4.10 Cost Profile of an ETF

The following are the costs typically associated with exchange-traded funds:

- **Trading costs:** These are the costs associated with purchasing underlying assets for an ETF or purchases/sales costs associated with rebalancing an ETF (e.g. broker costs, exchange or settlement fees).

- **Fees** e.g. fees to professionals, fees to index providers, listing fees, etc.

- **Operating Expenses:** Administrative expenses, marketing expenses, etc.

4.11 Tracking Error and Tracking Difference

Tracking error is the divergence in the returns of the ETF and the benchmark. It is computed as the standard deviation of Portfolio return and index return. Tracking Difference, on the other hand, is simply the difference between ETF return and Index return in a period.

Tracking error or tracking difference is an implication of the fact that ETFs are built on indices and indices are theoretical portfolios without the practical realities of actual portfolios e.g. costs, the timing of purchase and sales of securities, etc. (Cannon, Tracking error, the often-overlooked cost, September 2023). Seeing that the core objective of the ETF Fund Manager is to replicate the index as efficiently as possible, tracking errors/differences are thus very critical measures of the effectiveness of an ETF product. This is because the ETF product value proposition to the investor is exposure to the performance of an index.

Steps to computing ETF tracking error:

Formula: Tracking Error = Standard Deviation of (Portfolio Return – Index (benchmark return))

Please see below the steps for computing Tracking Error using Microsoft Excel. The brute force method is applied so all the steps are clearly seen:

Example 5:1 Computing Tracking Error Using MS Excel

- First tabulate the returns of the Portfolio and the returns of the benchmark for the applicable periods. This can be daily, monthly, quarterly, or yearly depending on the data available and the objective of the tracking error computation. Below, we are looking to compute the tracking error of a hypothetical portfolio versus a hypothetical benchmark over a six-month period using monthly return data:

Date	Portfolio Return (m/m)	Benchmark
Jan-24	10%	12%
Feb-24	9%	7%
Mar-24	5%	6%
Apr-24	7%	8%
May-24	4%	9%
Jun-24	5%	10%

- Subtract the benchmark return from the Portfolio Return to compute the Active or Excess Return

Date	Portfolio Return (m/m)	Benchmark	Active Return
Jan-24	10%	12%	-2%
Feb-24	9%	7%	2%
Mar-24	5%	6%	-1%
Apr-24	7%	8%	-1%
May-24	4%	9%	-5%
Jun-24	5%	10%	-5%

- Square the active return using the "caret" symbol ($^\wedge$) in Excel (i.e., Datacell$^\wedge$2) and then sum up all the squares (i.e., =SUM (datacell1:datracellN)

Date	Portfolio Return (m/m)	Benchmark	Active Return	Square of Active Return
Jan-24	10%	12%	-2%	0.04%
Feb-24	9%	7%	2%	0.04%
Mar-24	5%	6%	-1%	0.01%
Apr-24	7%	8%	-1%	0.01%
May-24	4%	9%	-5%	0.25%
Jun-24	5%	10%	-5%	0.25%
	Sum of Squares			0.60%

- Divide the sum of the squares by the number of periods minus 1 (N-1). In our example above, we have 6 periods

(January to June). Therefore N- 1 is 5. Then take the square root of the result using "=SQRT(number)" in Excel to give the monthly standard deviation of the portfolio against the benchmark.

- We can then annualise the monthly standard deviation figure to arrive at the annualised tracking error. We do this by multiplying the square root of 12. i.e. 3.46% * sqrt (12) giving an annualised tracking error of 12%.

Date	Portfolio Return (m/m)	Benchmark Return (m/m)	Active Return	Square of Active Return
Jan-24	10%	12%	-2&	0.04%
Feb-24	9%	7%	2%	0.04%
Mar-24	5%	6%	-1%	0.01%
Apr-24	7%	8%	-1%	0.01%
May-24	4%	9%	-5%	0.25%
Jun-24	5%	10%	-5%	0.25%
		Sum of Squares		0.60%
		Divided by N-1		0.12%
		Square root		3.46%

a shorter route would be to use the standard deviation function STDEV(dataset) in Excel.

How do we interpret the above? From the empirical rule in statistics, we learn that 68% of observed data points will lie inside one standard deviation of the mean (Frost, 2021). This means that there is a 68% probability in any year that the excess return of the above portfolio will be within 12% of the benchmark. This helps to have a sense of how much variation against the benchmark to expect.

For Exchange-Traded Funds or Index Managers, the tracking error should be as close to zero as possible but is usually between 1% and 2%. Active portfolios have higher tracking error profiles.

What can cause tracking error or tracking difference?

- **Cash drag:** Indices don't have cash holdings, but ETFs do. Cash can accumulate at intervals due to dividend payments, uninvested balances, and trading activity. The lag between receiving and reinvesting the cash can lead to a difference in performance known as cash drag. Dividend funds with high pay-out yields are most susceptible. **Cash drag can have a positive or negative impact on ETF performance, depending on the applicable cash yield versus applicable ETF portfolio return over a specific period.**

- **ETF costs:** ETFs have costs e.g. Trading Fees, Service Provider Fees, Regulatory Fees, and these can cause tracking errors. A simple example: If the HI index returns 20% in a year and all-in costs for running the ETF is 2%, then investors in the ETF will receive an 18% return. Tracking Difference for the period of 1 year is 2%.

- **Challenges with replication:** Benchmark composition vs portfolio composition: Sometimes it is difficult to achieve exact replication of a benchmark index at the exact price of each component security on the date of replication e.g. being able to match weightings during rebalancing especially when you have illiquid components.

- **Timing:** This is also relevant, especially during rebalancing. The time lag between when the rebalancing actions are published by the index provider and the time the ETF actually purchases or sells the relevant securities can cause a tracking error as the price of the relevant securities on the date the rebalancing is published by the index provider and the price on the date of actual purchase can differ.

In practice, Bond ETFs usually have higher tracking error profiles than Equity ETFs because most e.g., the Vetiva S&P Bond ETF, use sampling strategies or optimization (Cannon, 2023).

4.12   Index Replication Methods

As already established, the goal of an ETF is to replicate as closely as possible the performance of a reference index. There are various ways in which replication can be achieved. In Chapter 3, when we looked at the classification of ETFs by structure, we looked at physical and synthetic ETFs. This is also relevant when we look at the replication methods. Physically backed ETFs can either employ full replication or sampling whilst synthetic ETFs use the synthetic replication method.

4.12.1   Full Replication

This is when an ETF holds all the securities in an Index. This is the common replication method for equity ETFs with exposure to liquid indices e.g. the NGX30 ETF.

4.12.2   Sampling

Unfortunately, not all indices are liquid. Also, some indices have so many constituents, that it may be impractical to achieve full replication. In this instance, the Fund Manager may choose to purchase sample securities that seek to preserve the performance of the index. Sampling is usually used by fixed income funds and this approach comes with its own risk. The more aggressively you optimize a portfolio, the more its returns could vary from the index over time, either on the upside or downside.

Case Study: replicating the S&P Nigerian Sovereign Bond Index

The S&P/FMDQ Nigeria Sovereign Bond Index (NGN) tracks the performance of local currency denominated sovereign debt publicly issued by the government of Nigeria in its domestic market and was launched in 2014 (S&P Dow Jones Indices). In 2016, Vetiva Fund Managers Limited launched an ETF called the Vetiva S&P Nigerian Sovereign Bond ETF with the S&P/FMDQ Nigeria Sovereign Bond Index (NGN) as the benchmark index.

The Vetiva S&P Nigerian Sovereign Bond ETF is structured as an optimised ETF and invests only in a representative sample of the constituents of the benchmark index. When a security is included on the index, it stays in the index till maturity. The ETF, however, has a filter that excludes Bonds that have been "off the run" for more than 2 years from the portfolio and replaces them with similar "on-the-run" bonds to avoid holding illiquid assets.

"Off-the-run" Bonds are debt instruments issued by a government that are not the latest offering (of such debt instruments), whilst "On-the-run" Bonds are the most currently issued bonds (Corporate Finance Institute). Off-the-run Bonds are usually not as liquid as on-the-run bonds.

4.12.3   Synthetic replication

For physical replication, we have established that replication of the index is achieved by using the actual asset in an underlying portfolio. Synthetic replication, on the other hand, is when derivative products replicate the price movement or performance of an index or asset.

Key Takeaways

- *ETFs can take a variety of structures but are most commonly structured as open-ended funds.*

- *The Authorised Dealer is a Primary Market player and is responsible for ensuring continued liquidity for the ETF through the creation and redemption process and acts as Wholesaler of the ETF units.*

- *Choosing a benchmark index is an important activity for an ETF issuer as it determines the basis for the ETF portfolio composition.*

- *In Nigeria, ETFs are required to the registered with the Securities and Exchange Commission (SEC) and listed on an Exchange recognised by the SEC.*

- *Creation is the process of sourcing the underlying assets of an ETF as a basis for the creation of additional ETF units and an ETF redemption is the process of cancelling units of an ETF in exchange for the underlying assets.*

- *Through the ETF creation and Redemption process, additional units of an ETF are either be created or cancelled*

- *Tracking error is the divergence in the returns of the ETF and the benchmark.*

- *Investment in ETF units can either be cash (cash creation) or by relinquishing the underlying securities that represent the number of units required (In-specie creation).*

- *An active return is a difference between the benchmark and the actual return.*

- *From the empirical rule in statistics, we learn that 68% of observed data points will lie inside one standard deviation of the mean.*

- *In practice, Bond ETFs usually have higher tracking error profiles than Equity ETFs because most Bond ETFs use sampling strategies or optimization.*

- *Off-the-Run Bond are debt instruments issued by a government that are not the latest offering (of such debt instruments), whilst On-the-run Bonds are the most currently issued bonds of a specific tenor.*

<h1 style="text-align:center">Chapter 5</h1>

<h1 style="text-align:center">TRADING EXCHANGE-TRADED FUNDS</h1>

"There is a time to go long, a time to go short and a time to go fishing."
– Jesse Livermore

5.1 Introduction

As discussed in previous chapters, ETFs are traded on stock exchanges like any other security and can be accessed by purchasing units at any time during the trading period. This is quite different from traditional mutual funds, which can only be purchased via a fund manager based on prices that are determined at the end of the trading day. This unique feature of ETFs has essentially simplified access to pooled investment products.

5.2 Pricing of Exchange-Traded Funds (Market Price Vs. Net Asset Value)

Because ETFs trade on an exchange, the Market price of an ETF, during the trading period, is determined by demand and supply dynamics, like any other security. This means that if the demand for an ETF outstrips the available supply, then the price will rise and vice versa. This is in contrast with a mutual fund that is priced at the end of the trading day based on its Net Asset Value (NAV). The NAV of a fund is the value of the total assets of the fund less the total liabilities of the fund. The NAV of a fund is important because it is a standardized benchmark for determining fund performance. In most markets, including Nigeria, Fund Managers are expected to publish the NAV of ETFs being managed by them on a daily basis. In an ideal scenario, the Market Price of an ETF and the NAV should be the same. An ETF is said to be trading at a "premium" or "discount" depending on if the market price is higher or lower than its NAV.

One of the mechanisms that seek to ensure that the NAV of an ETF and the price of an ETF are as close as possible is the Redemption / Creation mechanism, which is carried out by the Authorised Dealer/Participant. In practice, when the supply of an ETF is thinning out, the Authorised Dealer creates more units to enhance supply and enable efficient price discovery.

Worked Example: An equity ETF, which tracks a broad market index, holds shares valued at ₦90million and cash of ₦10million. The ETF has unpaid Professional Fees and index licensing fees of ₦20million. If the ETF has 10million units outstanding, **what is the NAV per unit of the ETF?**

Computation: The NAV of an ETF is computed by valuing all the assets of the fund and deducting any liabilities e.g., accrued expenses, to arrive at a figure called NAV. The NAV figure is then divided by the number of outstanding units in the ETF to arrive at the NAV per unit of the Fund.

Workings:

Equities	₦90,000,000
Cash	₦10,000,000
Deduct: Liabilities:	₦20,000,000
ETF Net Asset Value (NAV):	₦80,000,000
ETF Net Asset Value per unit:	₦8 per Unit (i.e. ₦80,000,000 divided by 10,000,000 units)

5.3   ETF Trade Settlement

ETFs trade and settle on an Exchange just like any other listed security. Trade settlement refers to the transfer of securities from the seller to the buyer and cash from the buyer to the seller to consummate an executed trade. In the Nigerian equities market, the settlement cycle is T+3 i.e., transfer of securities and cash between the buyer and the seller is done 3 working days after the trade is consummated.

5.4   ETF Distributions

Because ETFs hold as their underlying assets, securities which may pay a return e.g. dividends from equities held by a Fund or coupon from fixed income securities held by a fund, an ETF, in line with its constitutional documents may choose to pay out this income to its unit holders. **This is called the ETF distribution.** Factors that may affect ETF distributions are nature of underlying asset class, frequency of distribution, ETF costs and Trust Deed provisions. It is important to note that ETF distributions may become taxable when received by Unit Holders.

5.5   Using ETFs to Execute Trading Strategies

There are different trading strategies employed by investors in seeking portfolio or investment returns. In this section, we explore how ETFs can be used to execute common trading strategies:

5.5.1   Trend trading or Trend following

Trend following or trend trading is a trading strategy in which an investor buys a security when its price trend is upwards or sells a security when its price trend is downwards, based on a prognosis that the price trend observed will be maintained. It can also be defined as a trading strategy that involves identifying the direction of a prevailing trend in the financial markets and then buying or selling selling securities in line with the identified trend (*www.capital.com*).

Illustration: ETFs can be used to take advantage of industry or sector trends. For example, if an upward trend is seen in the price of banking stocks and an investor believes this trend will be sustained, a Banking Sector ETF can be purchased to ride the trend.

5.5.2   Hedging

Hedging (sometimes called pairs trading) is a trading strategy that seeks to limit the risk of holding a security by investing in another security that will offset the price movements of the security. For example, an inverse ETF can be used to hedge the potential of losses on a long position.

5.5.3   Cost Averaging

Cost averaging is investing set amounts at regular intervals over time to manage timing risk and maintain a long term investment plan (*www.schwab.com*). This strategy is particularly useful for retail investors who are not very sophisticated, and evidence has shown that investors who have used this strategy have had positive outcomes (Brennan, 2005). However, it should be noted that one of the disadvantages of this strategy is that it can lead to losing some return potential. It also does not prevent losses (*www.fidelity.com*).

5.5.4 Swing Trading

This is a trading technique that relies on technical analysis to take advantage of short to medium-term capital appreciation potentials in a stock. From the trader's point of view, it entails employing relevant tools to identify when there is a likely upswing in the price of a stock (Mitchell, 2023). Swing trading is similar to day trading in that both trading strategies have a short-term focus, but day traders seek to take advantage of gains in stock prices within a trading day (Majaksi, 2023).

Some of the disadvantages of swing trading are:

- It can be difficult to execute in volatile markets and prices may not move as anticipated.

- It requires constant monitoring of market positions.

- It is a risky strategy and may lead to significant losses (Connell, 2023)

5.5.5 Sector Rotation

This is an active portfolio management strategy in which Portfolio investments in one sector is liquidated and the proceeds allocated to another sector to take advantage of positive sector trends or opportunities. For example, cyclical stocks perform better in a booming economy and as such if a recession is anticipated, an investor may decide to liquidate investments in sectors that are likely to be affected by a recession and invest the proceeds in other sectors that are defensive. Sector ETFs, which give exposure to certain sectors can be used to rotate from one sector to another depending on prevailing economic realities.

As with any trading strategy, Sector rotation comes with its own risks. Some analysts have questioned the effectiveness of sector rotation strategies, as it relies on the ability of the investor to accurately anticipate market trends thus exposing the portfolio to losses if the wrong calls are made.

5.6   Selecting an ETF to invest in

One of the global trends we have seen in recent years is some Fund Managers converting their mutual funds into ETFs. One of the key reasons asset managers are doing this is to take advantage of the strong growth profile of the ETF space. There are a number of factors to consider in choosing an ETF:

- Compare the associated costs and tracking efficiency of the proposed ETF with competing ETFs.

- Assess the underlying index to confirm if the desired exposure is captured by the Index.

- Consider the ETF structure adopted by the fund manager and assess associated risks or implications.

Conclusion

The global outlook for ETFs remains highly positive for a variety of reasons. ETFs have continued to grow in popularity due to their versatility, cost-efficiency, and ease of access, making them an increasingly integral part of investment portfolios worldwide. This scenario also holds true within the African context, especially in South Africa, which has the most developed ETF ecosystem. In West Africa, the adoption of Exchange-Traded Products has been relatively slow but with the commitment of stakeholders to capacity building both on the "buy" and "sell" sides of the market, I believe there is a huge room for growth for ETFs. This is primarily driven by the fact that the value proposition for ETFs is clear and undeniable.

As investors, particularly in Africa, seek more diversified and targeted exposures to various asset classes, sectors, and regions, the demand for innovative ETF products is expected to rise. This expanded use of ETFs in portfolios underscores the importance of having increased ETF listings in Africa, especially as it will provide investors with a broader range of options to better align their investments with specific goals and market conditions. Additionally, increasing the variety of ETF offerings can enhance market liquidity, reduce costs, and further democratize access to global investment opportunities. Therefore, a concerted effort to support the growth and availability of ETFs is essential for the continued evolution and resilience of the financial markets in West Africa and the wider African continent.

Key Takeaways

- *The NAV of a fund is the value of the total assets of the fund less the total liabilities of the fund.*

- *Trade settlement refers to the transfer of securities from the seller to the buyer and cash from the buyer to the seller to consummate an executed trade.*

- *Swing Trading is a trading technique that relies on technical analysis with the objective of taking advantage of short to medium term capital appreciation potentials in a stock.*

- *Sector ETFs, which give exposure to certain sectors can be used to rotate from one sector to another depending on prevailing economic realities.*

References

Blackrock Advisor Centre. (n.d.). Thematic ETFs. Blackrock Advisor Centre, pp. https://www.blackrock.com/us/financial-professionals/products/thematic-etfs

Blackrock (n.d.). Global Business Intelligence.

Brennan, M. J., Li, F. and Torous, W. N. (2005). Dollar cost averaging. *European Finance Review*, 9(4):509-535.

Cannon, I. O. (2023). Understanding ETFs, Tracking error, the often-overlooked cost. *Vanguard,* September.

Cannon, I. O. (2023). Tracking error, the often-overlooked cost. Understanding ETFs, https://corporate.vanguard.com, September.

Capital.com. (n.d.). What is trend trading?

Carlson, D. (n.d.). What to know about leveraged and inverse ETFs. *Britannica Money*, https://www.britannica.com

Charles Schwab Asset Management. (n.d.). What is fundamental index investing? https://www.schwabassetmanagement.com

Chen, J. (2020). Passive investing definition and pros & cons, vs. Active Investing. https://www.investopedia.com/terms/p/passiveinvesting, December 9.

Chen, J. (2022). Who was John Bogle? Vanguard Founder, Father of Indexing. *Investopedia.*

Chen, J. (2023). What is an index? Examples, How It's Used, and How to Invest. *Investopedia.*

Connell, B. O. (2023,). What is swing trading and is it right for you? *The Street*, pp. https://www.thestreet.com, February 9.

Connolly, T. P. (2013,). Does it matter how an index is put together? *CFA Institute Inside Investing*, pp. https://blogs. cfainstitute.org, May 8.

Consolidated SEC Rules, 2013

Corporate Finance Instittute. (n.d.). https://corporatefinance institute.com/resources/fixed-income/on-the-run-treasuries/.

Corporate Finance Institute. (n.d.). Smart Beta ETF.

Fidelity.com (2023). Pros and cons of dollar-cost. averaging. https://www.fidelity.com, May.

Frost, J. (2021). Empirical rule: Definition & formula. Statistics by Jim.

FTSE Russell (n.d.). FTSE RAFI Index Series.

GlobalX (n.d.). PAVE - U.S. Infrastructure development ETF. www.globalxetfs.com: https://www.globalxetfs.com/ funds/pave/

Investor.gov. (n.d.). Index funds. pp. https://www.investor. gov/introduction-investing/investing-basics/investment-products/mutual-funds-and-exchange-traded-4.

Jackson, A. and Curry, B. (2021, July 30). What is sector rotation? *Forbes ADVISOR*, Forbes.com, pp. https://www. forbes.com

Jark, D. (2024,). Benefits and risks of thematic ETFs. *Investopedia,* pp. https://www.investopedia.com, February 7

Johnson, S. (2024, February 19). Active ETF market share surges as growth accelerates. Financial Times, pp. https:// www.ft.com

Kamil Kaczmarski, S.F. (2010). The Renaissance of ETFS - Exchange-traded funds are fueling market opportunities. oliverwyman,https://www.oliverwyman.com.

Killa, S. (2024). Zacks Investment Research, https://www.nasdaq.com/articles/a-guide-to-the-10-most-popular-leveraged-etfs-1.

Majaksi, C. (2023). Day trading vs. swing trading: What's the difference? *Investopedia*, pp. https://www.investopedia.com, May 8.

McCullough, A.C. (2018). The fundamentals of fundamental indexing. *MorningStag* - ETF Education, pp. https://my.morningstar.com

Mitchell, C. (2023,). Swing trading: Definition and the pros and cons for investors. *Investopedia*, September 29

moneyterms.co.uk. (n.d.). Style Index. pp. https://moneyterms.co.uk/style-index

Murugaboopathy, P. (2024). Global passive equity funds' assets eclipsed active in 2023 for first time. Reuters.com.

Nasdaq. (2023). Currency ETFs: Benefits, risks, and examples. Hedder,https://www.nasdaq.com

NGX. (n.d.). Rules of listing of exchange traded-funds.

NGX Group. (n.d.). Market indices. p. https://ngxgroup.com/exchange/data/indices/.

Pisani, B. (2024, Feb 12). Bitcoin, AI and Magnificent 7: The emerging ETF trends as industry gathers for big conference. CNBC.com, pp. https://www.cnbc.com/2024/02/12/

PWC. (n.d.). ETF 2026, the next big leap.

PWC. (n.d.). ETFs 2028: shaping the Future. ttps://www.pwc.com

Reiff, N. (2024). What are actively managed ETFs and do they work? *Investopedia* https://www.investopedia.com/news

Riedl, D. (undated). Replication methods of ETFs. Just ETF, pp. https://www.justetf.com

S&P Dow Jones Indices. (n.d.). https://www.spglobal.com/

S&P Dow Jones Indices. (n.d.). https://www.spglobal.com/

S&P Dow Jones indices. (n.d.). Index lteracy. An investor's guide to Indices.

Saldanha, R. (2024, Jan 11). Share of U.S. active mutual fund AUM could drop to 17%. *MorningStar*, pp. https://www.morningstar.ca/ca/news

Salvucci, J. (Updated 2022). What is an inverse ETF? Definition, purpose and examples. *TheStreet*, https://www.thestreet.com/dictionary/inverse

Schwab.com. (2017). What is dollar cost averaging? https://www.schwab.com

Statistica (n.d.). Largest ETFS market. https://www.statista.com/

Statista Research Department (2024). ETFs - statistics & facts. *Statista Research Department*.

Toronto Stock Exchange. (2020). Toronto Stock Exchange - ETF Report (Q1 2020).

Trading Brokers. (2023, August 28). Pros and cons of swing trading. *Trading Guides*, pp. https://tradingbrokers.com

Wikipedia. (n.d.). Capitalisation weighted index. pp. https://en.wikipedia.org/

Wikipedia. (n.d.). SPDR S&P 500 Trust ETF. https://en.wikipedia.org

Wikipedia. (n.d.). Trend following. https://en.wikipedia.org/

Index

www.ingramcontent.com/pod-product-compliance
Lightning Source LLC
Chambersburg PA
CBHW031157160726
47992CB00006B/2487